ARCHITECTURAL DESIGN
Vol 68 No 9/10 September-October 1998

EDITORIAL OFFICES:
42 LEINSTER GARDENS, LONDON W2 3AN
TEL: + 44 171 262 5097 FAX: + 44 171 262 5093

EDITOR: Maggie Toy
DEPUTY EDITOR: Ellie Duffy
DESIGN: Mario Bettella and Andrea Bettella/Artmedia
ADVERTISEMENT SALES: Nicky Douglas

CONSULTANTS: Catherine Cooke, Terry Farrell, Kenneth Frampton, Charles Jencks, Heinrich Klotz, Leon Krier, Robert Maxwell, Demetri Porphyrios, Kenneth Powell, Colin Rowe, Derek Walker

SUBSCRIPTION OFFICES:

UK: JOHN WILEY & SONS LTD
JOURNALS ADMINISTRATION DEPARTMENT
1 OAKLANDS WAY, BOGNOR REGIS
WEST SUSSEX, PO22 9SA, UK
TEL: 01243 843272 FAX: 01243 843232
E-mail: cs-journals@wiley.co.uk

USA AND CANADA:
JOHN WILEY & SONS, INC
JOURNALS ADMINISTRATION DEPARTMENT
605 THIRD AVENUE
NEW YORK, NY 10158
TEL: + 1 212 850 6645 FAX: + 1 212 850 6021
CABLE JONWILE TELEX: 12-7063
E-mail: subinfo@wiley.com

ANNUAL SUBSCRIPTION RATES 1998: UK £90.00, student rate: £65.00; Outside UK US$145.00, student rate: $105.00. AD is published six times a year. Prices are for six issues and include postage and handling charges. Periodicals postage paid at Jamaica, NY 11431. Air freight and mailing in the USA by Publications Expediting Services Inc, 200 Meacham Ave, Elmont, Long Island, NY 11003.

SINGLE ISSUES: UK £18.99; Outside UK $29.95. Order two or more titles and postage is free. For orders of one title please add £2.00/$5.00. To receive order by air please add £5.50/$10.00.

POSTMASTER: send address changes to AD, c/o Publications Expediting Services Inc, 200 Meacham Ave, Elmont, Long Island, NY 11003.

Printed in Italy. All prices are subject to change without notice.
[ISSN: 0003-8504]

CONTENTS

ARCHITECTURAL DESIGN **MAGAZINE**

Pneu World, *Architectural Design*, 1968

ARCHITECTURAL DESIGN **PROFILE** NO 135

EPHEMERAL/PORTABLE ARCHITECTURE

Robert Kronenburg • *Vladimir Krstic* • **Henrietta Palmer** • *Mark Prizeman* • **Nicholas Goldsmith** • *Joep van Lieshout* • **Torsten Schmiedeknecht** • *Haus-Rucker-Co* • **Günter Zamp Kelp** • *Toyo Ito* • **Apicella Associates** • *Mark Fisher* • **FTL Happold** • *Branson Coates Architecture* • **Wendy Gunn and Gavin Renwick**

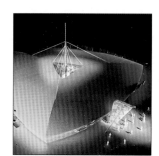

Apicella Associates, The Communicator

Toyo Ito, Shimosuwa Municipal Museum, Nagano

AD

Pneu world

The front cover of
AD *June 1968*

PNEU WORLD
ARCHITECTURAL DESIGN, JUNE 1968

You name it, someone is blowing it up right now, but it isn't quite as new as is sometimes made out. The basic patents on balloon-type envelopes go back to John Boyd Dunlops' first tyres and beyond; on air-supported buildings they go back to F W Lanchester in 1917. The first great monument of environmental wind-baggery, the US Atomic Energy Commission's mobile theatre designed by Victor Lundy and Walter Bird, has been on the road for a decade.

What is new is a confluence between changing taste and advances in plastic technology. The taste that has been turned off by the regular rectangular format of official modern architecture and Bauhaus-revival modern-antique furniture, is turned right on by the apparent do-it-yourself rotentialities of low-pressure inflatable technology. Transparent Mylar and related materials are temptingly easy to work with, and the inflating mechanism need be no more complex than a domestic vacuum cleaner.

From Reyner Banham's 'Monumental wind-bags', *New Society*, 18 April, 1968.

To complement the themes of portability and ephemerality, *AD* steps back 30 years to June 1968, with the following pages reproduced from an issue that was devoted entirely to pneumatic architecture. Under the editorship of Monica Pidgeon, and with Robin Middleton as technical editor, 'Pneu World' kicked off with a review entitled 'When is Art, Art?' by Jasia Reichardt, which discussed among other things Utopie's 'Structures Gonflables' exhibition at the Museum of Modern Art in Paris, and the work of Christo and Charles Eames. This was followed by a manifesto by Utopie (Jean Aubert, Jean-Paul Jungmann, Antoine Stinco and Hubert Tonka), who were introduced to their first British audience as 'a French student group critical of the contemporary architectural and urban scene'.

AA students Johnny Devas, David Harrison, Mike Davies, Dave Martin and Simon Connolly were responsible for putting together the title article, which was a sort of step-by-step guide to the principles and categories of inflatable architecture. This they introduced with the opening quotation from Reyner Banham's essay 'Monumental Windbags'. Realised inflatable structures from archi-tects such as Frei Otto and Buckminster Fuller were shown alongside ground-breaking project work from students and practitioners in the UK (including Mike Webb, Peter Murray, and Piers Gough). In addition, the authors gathered together the latest developments in materials and structures from the aeronautics and space industries, as well as the military and commercial industry.

The main feature covered projects by Utopie architects Aubert, Jungmann, and Stinco, and the issue was rounded-off with a consumer piece on where and what to purchase in the way of inflatable furniture. Also included was a stop-press on the death of Sigfried Gideon, author of *Space, Time and Architecture*. The classic image of the issue though has to be the picture of a young Piers Gough putting the finishing touches to his AA competition-winning inflatable structure 'Mother of the Arts'.

Ellie Duffy

The frontis image from AD *June 1968*

Pneu world

Simon Conolly
Mike Davies
Johnny Devas
David Harrison
Dave Martin
*Students at the Architectural Association
School of Architecture, London*

Pneumatic principles have already been widely adopted and accepted; from sailing ships, lilos and car tyres to storage tanks. When used for structures pneumatics fall into two basic categories: single-layer air-supported and air-inflated structures.

SINGLE-LAYER AIR-SUPPORTED

A flexible membrane is supported in tension by a compressed fluid which reacts against a loadbearing surface (usually the ground). The used volume is usually at a slightly higher pressure than that outside – 1/500th atmosphere. An analysis of soap bubbles is relevant to the study of these types of membrane under uniform stress. Basic principles may be applied even without adherence to pure theoretical geometry (figs 3, 5). Airlocks are generally required but cause limitations of entry, exit, and circulation.

A constant air input (vital to structural stability) is required. The concept of the pneumatic structure as a packaged and instantly inflatable volume is often incompatible with the practical problems of relating the structure to a particular site. With single-layer structures anchoring and layout considerations are critical as the membrane stress must be distributed around the perimeter and air sealing ensured.

The single-layer principle has been applied primarily where shelter and little else is required – radomes, warehouses, school enclosures etc. Present applications exploit the inflatable as an easily transported, quickly erected volume package,

1 Instantly inflatable life jacket
2 Man descending at 25 f.p.s.
3 Project for membrane spanning amorphous plan
4 Car tyre. Around 25 p.s.i.
5 Donald Duck in New York

but once initial inflation is complete, they take on the role of static structures at a fixed location. Once they are erected, extension can generally be achieved only by deflation of the total structure and addition of extra modules. Low cost, even accepting a short life span (7-10 years average), implies a genuine throw-away product.

AIR-INFLATED STRUCTURE
A membrane completely enclosing compressed air which may be analysed under two main headings.

Cushion (fig 6)

Double-layer (fig 7)
In this category, apertures can be where you want them. Greater thermal and acoustic control is possible. Self-deployment is a particular advantage.
The structure does not require an air seal to the ground; inflation is rapid.
A relatively small air input is required for rigidity and segments may be added without altering the initial construction (figs 8, 9). A higher pressure is required; hence a higher performance is needed for joints, seals, and the membrane itself.

INFLATED RIBBED STRUCTURES
High pressure tube frames (figs 10, 11). Freedom of structural form.
The membrane is independent of the rib structure (figs 12, 13). It can be changed easily, allowing greater control of heat, light, and sound. At present it is difficult to add to a pressure tube structure. A kit of standard joints and rib sections may resolve the difficulty.
Inflation is instant. Initial air input is very small. High pressure, however, requires high performance joints, seals, and fabric. Self-deployment – the pop-up package.

BASIC AMENITY
Pneumatics (as packaged volumes) offer a choice as to whether a structure is there or not, but once erected, the structure is inflexible in terms of physical response, apart from a limited expansion by addition. The life-raft is a sophisticated instant structure. Could instantly inflatable volume packages be clipped to existing structures to respond to immediate volume-change requirements? What if there were a common material with the elastic properties of a toy balloon?

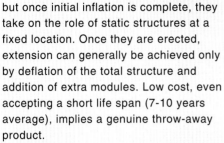
6

7

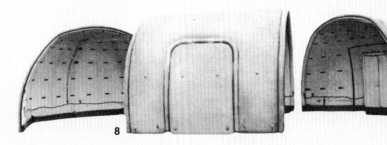
8

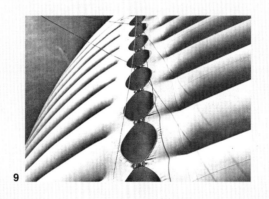
9

10

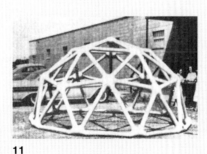
11

12

6 Cushion covering over US Atomic Energy Commission exhibition
7 American Airlines Astrosphere. 100ft diameter, 45ft (high) dual walled dome built up of segments in which the two layers are joined in continuous horizontal seams. An air-gap at either end of each seam allows a segment to be inflated as a single element. Total inflation time 2-3 hrs
8 Sections can be added to 'Airmat' shelter designed on a basic module. Additions, if conforming to standard configurations, can take place on site
9 Detail of segmental military shelter showing external joint between segments and continuous horizontal seams joining inner and outer skins
10 Inflated ribbed principle
11 Experimenal dome with pheumatically tensed cylindrical struts
12 Radome erecting device, using high pressure tube frame

HIGH AMENITY

What can pneumatics offer in furthering the relationship between environmental control and the individual?

They could act as sophisticated mechanisms for controlling heat, light and sound, rather than a basic enclosure with control equipment inside.

The most sophisticated work in this field has been carried out by Nikolaus Laing, who has designed a multi-layer skin system incorporating heat-reflecting and heat-absorbing elements, which can be dynamically controlled solely by air pressure (fig 14). These regulate precisely air temperature, light, humidity, rainfall and air circulation, with solar radiation as the only energy input, except for negligible amounts of subsidiary energy for control purposes (air pressure to deploy the membrane elements).

Tropical climates can be created in Newfoundland, and zero temperatures in the Sahara . . . extending the human habitat beyond the presently favoured regions.

There could be one cheap and portable element combining all the functions of the usual climatic control environmongery.

If a dynamic air-pocket system can regulate solar radiation, heat loss, and humidity, could it not act also as a communications and entertainment medium and a mood stimulus (figs 15-17) thus providing a more beneficial interaction between the individual and his immediate environment.

The potential of pneumatics as instant variable volume packages capable of providing high control and response to demand, could realize the concept of nomadic existence as elements within a kit of other high amenity systems . . . jet-pack, hoverdeck, air-floor, cybernet, energy sponge, power pack, exoskeleton (what about the camel?), and cheese spread. Hard and soft utilibles for the developing nomad.

In order to relate the current vocabulary of communications equipment, pneumatics elements, flexible frameworks, travel hardware, etc, to our speculations and the immediate future, we are presently working on a high-amenity amoebic kit with which we shall travel Europe. The single element enclosure becomes irrelevant when thinking in terms of a kit of metamorphic parts, and maybe the kit itself becomes transmutable when the parts are less than tangible.

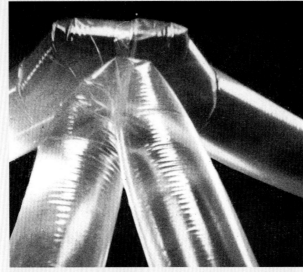

13

14

15

16

17

13 Four-way ribbed frame joint in polythene tube. Covering removed
14 Application of Laing's climatic control system to a city project
15 Mother of the Arts, by Piers Gough, AA
16, 17 Authors' experiments

Clothing for living in – or if it wasn't for my suitaloon I would have to buy a house

The space suit could be identified as a minimal house. In the previous cushicle (*AD* 11/66, p576), the environment for the rider was provided by the cushicle – a mechanism like a car. In this project the suit itself provides all the necessary services, the cushicle being the source of (a) movement, (b) a larger envelope than the suit can provide, (c) power. Each suit has a plug serving a similar function as the key to your front door. You can plug into your friend and you will both be in one envelope, or you can plug into any envelope, stepping out of your suit, the suit being left clipped onto the outside ready to step into when you leave. The plug also serves as a means of connecting envelopes together to form larger spaces.

The cushicle shown is for one rider only; various models of cushicle envelope and suit would of course be available ranging from your super sports to family models. *Mike Webb*

1 Suitaloon, a development of the cushicle
2 Flooring box partially unfolded
3 Flooring panel fully formed with living envelope partially inflated
4 Flooring panel fully formed, living envelope fully inflated and inhabitant plugged in at power connexion point in preparation for exploded entry
5 Suitaloon with rider in pressurized service suite in travelling position
6 Suitaloon pivoted to deposit rider
7 Boy meets girl, both in high-pressurized service suit. Plugging-in their respective power points results in an explosive merger

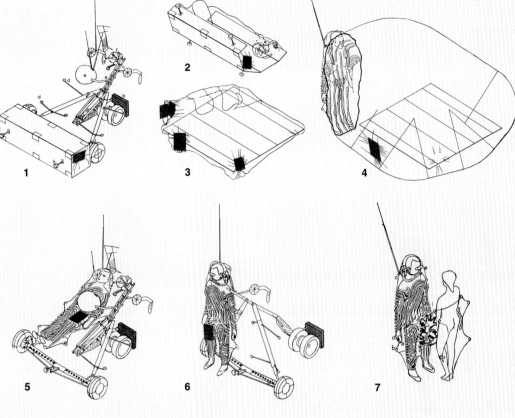

Travelling hall

A transportable exhibition hall divided into two separate areas, the one for large-scale exhibitions, the other for documentation and detailed information. The halls are formed of portions of spheres inflated internally to a pressure of about 50 gr/m². They are separated by an entrance chamber or lobby acting as an air-lock. Inflated ribs form the base of the two halls and serve to stabilize both the shape and the structure. The ribs are secured by cables to the tented covering of the whole, which is laid out and positioned in part by means of water-filled balloons, in part by the transportation trucks, before the membranses of the halls themselves are inflated. No anchorage to the ground is necessary. *A Stinco*

1 Detail of model
2 Exhibition cases set up, entrance lobbies installed
3 Supporting spheres fully inflated
4 Ground plan of hall
5 Exploded diagram of halls, B documentation, A exhibition

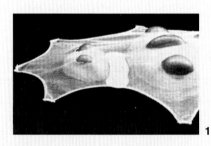

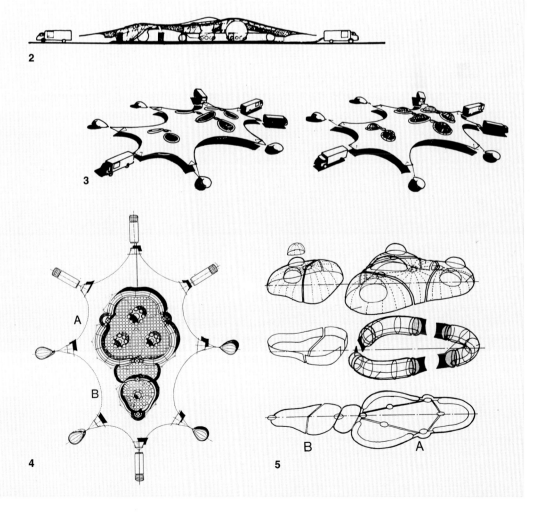

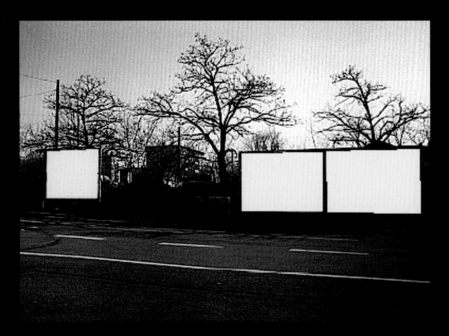 

TORSTEN SCHMIEDEKNECHT

CITYSCAPES
Darmstadt, Germany

'Cityscapes' was the response to a fine arts competition brief for Mühltal, Germany, in 1995. The project, which was awarded the first prize, addresses two main issues: the ephemeral nature of the space that is covered by advertising in the city, and the way in which the city dweller has accepted the occupation of visual public space by images that communicate abstract commands to consume.

The question is what the public is willing to accept as occupier of the visual public realm. Are we more willing to be seduced by, and to accept, the messages of advertising and its occupation of large amounts of space within the city, rather than encounter and be challenged by unknown means of visual communication, such as the superimposition of artistic icons and the questioning of our ways of perceiving the urban environment?

Advertising boards are fascinating in terms of their nature. Although they often last for decades in the same place, their appearance is inherently ephemeral, for the messages they communicate are constantly changing.

Along main roads in Spain or Portugal, especially near big cities like Barcelona or Lisbon, the steel structures bearing the huge advertising posters have developed their own typology: they are unique carriers of two-dimensional messages aimed at the motorist. In the open land-scape these structures act as mediators of scale between the city or mountain in the background, and the speed with which the motorist is travelling past.

We do not often perceive the beauty of the structures that relate the images because our eyes are transfixed by the advertised message. Similarly, in cities where space is precious we forget what is hidden behind the boards that have

become our facades. The carriers for the advertising in the city are our buildings, or the public space that relates to them. What is Piccadilly Circus like behind Fuji and Coca Cola? For long, architects like Jean Nouvel or Herzog & de Meuron have taken these phenomena into account by designing tailor-made facades that incorporate advertising.

The Cityscapes project was designed to take place in the city of Darmstadt in Germany, which has 140,000 inhabitants and approximately 135 large-scale advertising boards. All of the large advertising boards in the city would be rented for 10 consecutive days, during which time they would be painted yellow. The project was to start on a Monday, having been executed the night before. If possible, small and mid-size boards would also be incorporated.

The desired effect was that the whole

city would appear in a glow of yellow two-dimensional signs communicating only one thing: the colour yellow. As in the Venturian sense, the two-dimensional sign remains architecture only in that its message is distinctly abstract.

Advertising spaces are surfaces for the communication of authorised messages, as opposed to graffiti that has no official 'permission'. However, it is interesting to note how rarely advertising boards are subjected to graffiti, considering the comparatively high percentage of their occurrence.

Cityscapes would thus deliberately occupy these spaces and offer mono-chrome surfaces to look at. The intention was to manipulate and vary the surface qualities of the painted boards. Depending on the location and texture, the boards would be taken over by the public who would leave their own 'unauthorised' marks

on them. After the 10-day period it was likely that none of the boards would retain their original appearance. The conjunction of abstract image and texture was meant to encourage people to experience their built environment in a different way: people would be inspired by the textures or just add imagery.

The notion of textures and their signifi-cance within the public realm is linked inherently with the problem of scale. As with the virtual ephemeral image on the TV screen, we do not relate direct tactile qualities to an advertising board because its communication is purely visual. How-ever, unlike the televised image, the advertising board has a texture. A large advertising board appears as one unit and therefore most advertising is two-dimensional with a flat surface. This flatness has a quality of its own because it captures the dirt, the smell, the wetness

or dryness of the urban fabric.

Advertising boards are often mounted in front of brick buildings or structures of a more detailed texture. Thus we are confronted with a change of scale that is almost cut-like. 'Cityscapes' attempted to use these cuts in the urban fabric as a means of raising awareness of a more sensual encounter with the city and its textured surfaces. Through the coming together of different surface qualities and scales on and around the yellow boards of 'Cityscapes', the notion of the tactile encounter with the city would become evident.

The main impact of the project would occur after its 10 day existence. The boards would change their appearance for the city dweller, who would perceive the spaces along main roads or surround-ing junctions in a different way once the first cigarette advertisement reappeared.

Working with copper is always something special. Copper's excellent workability and its unique surfaces give you the freedom to develop architectural ideas that really work. TECU® products, available in all of copper's natural surfaces, are the perfect choice for your individualised roofing and façades.

With its Shingles System, the TECU® series features a special copper solution for both fast and economic roof work and wall cladding: The large shingles are easy to work with, making for extremely accurate and flexible application. They are available in all TECU® surfaces: classical copper red, oxidised brown, patinated green or tin grey.

true to form

TECU® Shingles – for true to form architectural design

KME – Technical
Customer Service:
Tel. +49 541 321- 43 23
Fax +49 541 321- 40 30

KM Europa Metal AG
Postfach 33 20
D - 49023 Osnabrück

Internet
http: // www.kme.de

Product information:
KME UK Ltd.
Goldthorn Road
Kidderminster
GB - Worcestershire DY 117 JD
Tel. + 44 1562 82 01 10
Tel. + 44 1562 74 12 11
Fax + 44 1562 51 53 81

TECU®-Classic
TECU®-Oxid
TECU®-Patina
TECU®-Zinn
 **TECU**®-Shingles

TECU®
Creative coverage.

Verona was commissioned in 1974 by the Ottolenghi family, who were friends of the architect. In this book Dal Co uses material from the Scarpa archives to reconstruct the process of design. Photographs of the exterior and interior are presented alongside an extensive collection of preliminary design sketches to provide a clear record of Scarpa's design intentions.

Antoine Predock's Turtle Creek House near Dallas is beautifully presented, with the focus of this book being a photographic record of the interior and exterior, preceded by presentation elevations, sections and axonometrics. A few early design sketches accompany Antoine Predock's introduction, in which he explains the requirements of the clients and his approach to their brief.

Mark Mack's Stremmel House rests on a plinth on an exposed hillside site overlooking the twin cities of Reno and Sparks, Nevada. Inspired by a concept sketch from Walter Pichler – an image of the 'sheltered mind and the unsheltered body' – the house was designed to accommodate the client's extensive collection of contemporary art , and to respond to the high-desert environment and climate.

This book benefits from the inclusion of tiny, iconic plans adjacent to captions, which allow readers to locate themselves in the house and identify the precise viewpoint of each photograph.

A James Speyer: Architect, Curator, Exhibition Designer, *John Vinci, The University of Chicago Press (Illinois), colour and b/w ills, PB, $25*
In his role as curator of 20th-century painting and sculpture at the Art Institute of Chicago, for which he is best remembered, Speyer not only oversaw over 125 exhibitions during his 25-year tenure (including Jean Dubuffet, Edward Hopper, Max Ernst, Marcel Duchamp etc) but he built up a fine collection of paintings and sculpture for the Institute's permanent collection. With his retrospective of Mies van der Rohe in 1968, Speyer also introduced a programme of architectural exhibitions. His design input was also remarkable: as Vinci reveals, in certain exhibitions the relationship of the design to the displayed works of art seemed to take on a life of its own.

This book celebrates the many qualities that Speyer lent to the field of design and architecture. An essay by Franz Schulze charts his life and career, examining the significance of his move from Harvard to Chicago in the 30s, where he became the first American graduate student of Mies van der Rohe and returned there to teach under Mies in the 40s. At the same time, Speyer designed glass and steel houses in Chicago and Pittsburgh. While offering an interesting insight into the curatorial field, the book also includes accounts from Speyer's friends and colleagues appreciating different aspects of the life and work of this modest luminary.

Design in the Fifties: When Everyone Went Modern, *George H Marcus, Prestel (Munich, New York), colour and b/w ills, PB, £16.95*
Modern design caught on quickly in the wake of the Second World War. A fresh start was needed and the accent was on progress and all things modern. This is exemplified by Edgar Kaufmann Junior's 'Twelve Precepts of Modern Design' (published by the Museum of Modern Art, NY in 1950), which included such statements as: 'Modern design should take advantage of new materials and techniques and develop familiar ones'; 'Modern design should be simple, its structure evident in its appearance, avoiding extraneous enrichment'; and 'Modern design should serve as wide a public as possible, considering modest needs and limited costs no less challenging than the requirements of pomp and luxury'.

Dream homes, prefabricated buildings, machines for living in, quirky biomorphic furniture, objects, and architecture (eg Eero Saarinen's TWA airline building, Le Corbusier's sculptural pilgrimage chapel, Ronchamp) – all attested to an unbridled creativity that is well documented in this appealing and very readable volume. It entertains us with adverts from the period, which convey the spirit of the time. 'Zanuso's Anthropomorphism in Foam', for example, features a selection of chairs that are, really, 'foam rubber shaped to the human figure' ('The Lady' style of chair is, of course, 'young and elegant'). The publication of this book is timely, tapping into the wave of nostalgia for 50s design that is, even in the most modernist environments, creeping back in the form of curvy 'Smeg' fridges in ice-cool pastel shades.

The Tudor & Jacobean Country House: A Building History, *Malcolm Airs, foreword by Mark Girouard, Sutton Publishing (Stroud), PB, £12.99*
First published in 1995, this paperback edition (produced in association with the National Trust) provides a well-informed background to the country house and its builders, focusing on an era that was one of the most exciting in terms of architectural development, and which

Reviews

culminated in the works of Shakespeare, Ben Jonson and Inigo Jones.

In the 16th century, before Inigo Jones established a more intellectual design approach, the treatment of Renaissance architecture in England tended to be more whimsical and decorative, evident in the 'dressing up' of facades with Renaissance features that were likely to have been seen and copied from a house elsewhere rather than the product of precise drawings.

The author's primary sources are the building accounts of houses and the builders' correspondence. His lively coverage not only charts the patrons' motives for building, the sites, designers, the process and expenditure, materials (and their transportation) etc, but also explores the working conditions of the labourers and their home life. The text thus allows an overall picture of the building trade to emerge. It is interspersed throughout with plans, engravings and photographs of varying quality.

Bridgescape: The Art of Designing Bridges,
Frederick Gottemoeller, John Wiley & Sons, (Chichester), 276pp, b/w ills, HB, $49.95
Bridges have been the subject of increased attention, as attested by the number of exhibitions and the spate of publications in recent years. This handy volume seeks to clarify the the creative process by highlighting the fundamental elements of the bridge (line, form and site intervention), in addition to concerns relating to colour, texture and ornamentation.

Gottemoeller is well-versed in the art of bridge design as a result of various collaborative efforts in the field. His experience as an architect-engineer, urban designer and teacher, is evident in his straightforward approach to the subject, guiding the reader through the basics and practical procedures of bridge design, to the design language and construction. Drawings and photographs also assist in communicating the way in which the bridge's appearance can be enhanced by a few essential factors.

Often neglected in bridge engineering is the aesthetic dimension, which is central to this study. Gottemoeller emphasises the inextricable link between architecture and engineering and the need for a happy medium. As Alberti wrote in the *Art of Building* (1486), ' . . . to build something praised by the munificent, yet not rejected by the frugal, is the province of an artist of experience, wisdom, and thoughtful deliberation.'

Towards a New Museum, *Victoria Newhouse, The Monacelli Press (New York), 288pp, colour and b/w ills, PB, £27.50*
The 20th century has witnessed a significant increase in the number of museums, particularly in recent decades. In the last 30 years, for example, more than 600 new museums have emerged in the USA alone. In her analysis of the 'new' museum, the author categorises the variety of conceptual and design approaches in a coherent manner, tackling the subject matter typologically.

The chapters are devoted to aspects of the museum, such as sacred space, the monographic museum, the museum as subject matter (artists' museums and their alternative spaces), the museum as entertainment – well illustrated by the fantastical Groninger Museum – and the museum as environmental art. Each section contains a short introduction and features notable case studies, many of which will be familiar to the reader since a considerable proportion are designed by well-known architects.

While architects need to strike a balance between the container and the contained, the impact of the expressionist potential of architecture on the museum can be felt by the close of the book, which culminates, unsurprisingly, in the definitive work of Frank Gehry. Like a Hermann Finsterlin sketch brought to life, Gehry's sculptural, curvilinear museums in Minnesota, Bilbao and Samsung display a sophisticated command of materials and slick confidence that has come to characterise much of late 20th-century architecture. His work is preceded by, and encourages comparison with Daniel Libeskind's Jewish Museum Extension in Berlin, which is a compelling exercise in significant form. The jagged geometry of this museum-vehicle is laden with symbolic resonance, voids and scars. Curiously, there is no mention here of Libeskind's recent project for the V&A Museum in London.

Overall, the content of the book is well-organised and stimulating. Moreover, the central task of identifying architecture as an integral part of the art experience is communicated with great clarity. Wisely, Newhouse also raises key issues relating to the physical expansion of the building fabric, highlighting the problems that have occurred at museums such as the MoMA and the Metropolitan Museum of Art, in contrast to examples of 'wings that fly' such as Jim Stirling's Staatsgalerie in Stuttgart and the much debated Sainsbury Wing at the National Gallery in London.

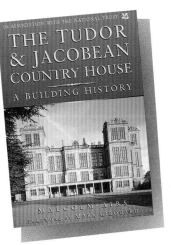

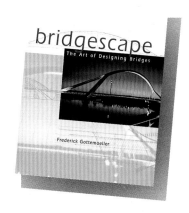

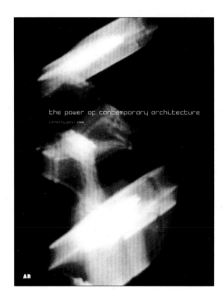

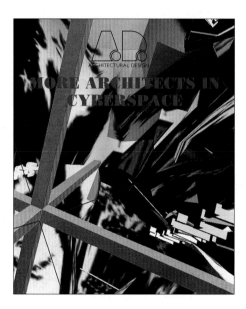

A HISTORY OF GRAPHIC DESIGN

THIRD EDITION

PHILIP B MEGGS

This unrivalled classic on the history of graphic design is essentially a Janson's History of Art for the graphic design world. The first edition of this book led to the creation of a new core course in the graphic design curriculum.

Since the second edition was published in 1991, the world of computer-generated graphics had changed dramatically. This revised, up-to-date edition is therefore extensive. Filled with informative text and a large variety of visual examples, it features everything from the invention of writing and graphic communications in Ancient Egypt to modern corporate identity and computer graphics. It also includes new information on computer graphics and non-Western graphic design.

- Affords a unique insight into graphic design
- Written by a leading scholar in the field
- Features over 370 colour images
- Appeals to students of design, professional designers and art historians

HB 0471 29198 6, 216 x 279, 512pp, £50.00: August 1998

THE POWER OF CONTEMPORARY ARCHITECTURE

PETER COOK AND NEIL SPILLER

A stunning directory for contemporary architects, educators and students: this book compares and contrasts the fashions and conceptual developments of architects from around the world and is a must-have for anyone in need of a clear overview of styles and their derivatives.

The book contains around 36 lecture-derivatives by influential architects of a generation that collaboratively demonstrates the power of conceptual architecture throughout the world. The collection opens with a foreword by Brian Clarke, and is introduced by essays from the editors.

- Famous and influential contributors
- Demonstrates schools of thought development in architecture
- Wide international appeal

PB 0471 98419 1, 217 x 279, 128pp, approx Y45.00 £24.95 $45.00: December 1998

MORE ARCHITECTS IN CYBERSPACE

Guest-edited by Neil Spiller
AD PROFILE 136

Following on from the success of *Architects in Cyberspace*, published three years ago, this subsequent issue of *Architectural Design* not only charts the progress of top cyberspace architects, but also features a number of new players in the field. In addition to the intriguing collection of essays and projects, it includes a review of the 1997 Paris Cyberspace exhibition, putting it firmly at the cutting edge of this ever-expanding subject.

- Extensively illustrated in colour
- Appeals to architects, architecture students, educators, computer fanatics, planners, and individuals with a general interest in cyberspace

PB 0471 98467 1, 305 x 250, 112pp, Y32.50 £ 18.99 $32.50: November 1998

ARCHITECTURAL DESIGN
SUBSCRIPTION RATES

SIX DOUBLE ISSUES A YEAR

Architectural Design continues to publish a vigorous and wide-ranging treatment of architectural trends of topical importance. Frequently in the forefront of theoretical developments in the architectural field, a main aim of *AD* has been to engender an awareness of philosophy in art and architecture whilst always maintaining a pluralist approach. The treatment of the divergent subjects examined over the years has had a profound impact on the architectural debate, making *AD* an invaluable record for architectural thinking, criticism and achievements.

ARCHITECTURAL DESIGN SUBSCRIPTION RATES		
	UK	OUTSIDE UK
Full rate	£90.00	US$145.00
Student rate	£65.00	US$105.00
Airmail prices on application		

PRICES REFLECT RATES FOR A 1998 SUBSCRIPTION
AND ARE SUBJECT TO CHANGE WITHOUT NOTICE

Back numbers are available. For more information see over.

FORTHCOMING ISSUES

VOL 6811/12/98............................More Architects in Cyberspace
VOL 69 1/2/99...Des-res Architecture

Presents the latest architectural explorations in cyberspace

Explores the notion of 'the house' in architecture

VOL 69 3/4/99..Sci-fi Architecture
VOL 69 5/6/99................................Infomatics and Architecture

Please complete and return this form with your payment (to be made payable to John Wiley & Sons Ltd) or credit card authority direct to:

OUTSIDE UK Subscriptions (US $)
John Wiley & Sons, Inc
Journals Administration Department
605 Third Avenue
New York, NY 10158, USA
Tel: 212 850 6645; Fax: 212 850 6021
Cable Jonwile; Telex: 12-7063
E-mail: subinfo@jwiley.com

UK Subscriptions (£)
John Wiley & Sons Ltd
Journals Administration Department
1 Oldlands Way, Bognor Regis
West Sussex, PO22 9SA, UK
Tel: 01243 843272; Fax: 01243 843232
E-mail: cs-journals@wiley.co.uk

ACADEMY EDITIONS
A division of John Wiley & Sons
42 Leinster Gardens, London W2 3AN Tel: 0171 262 5097 Fax: 0171 262 5093

ARCHITECTURAL DESIGN

☐ I wish to subscribe to *Architectural Design* at the full rate
☐ I wish to subscribe to *Architectural Design* at the student rate
☐ I wish to subscribe for a friend to *Architectural Design* at the full rate
☐ I wish to subscribe for a friend to *Architectural Design* at the student rate
.... **Starting date:** ☐ From issue 1/2/98
            ☐ From next available issue

.... **Payment enclosed by Cheque/ Money Order/ Drafts**
    Value/Currency £/US$...
.... **Please charge £/US$.........................to my credit card**

Account no:

Expiry date:

Card: Visa/Amex/Mastercard/Eurocard (*delete as applicable*)

Cardholder's signature...
Cardholder's name...
Address...
....**Post/Zip Code:**........................

Recipient's name..
Address...
....**Post/Zip Code:**........................

Please indicate your job title

☐ Architect
☐ Landscape Architect
☐ Architectural Technician/Assistant
☐ Surveyor
☐ Building Services Engineer
☐ Town Planner
☐ Interior Designer
☐ Designer
☐ Building Contractor
☐ Property Developer
☐ Student (*state college/university below*)
☐ Other (*state below*)

Please indicate your organisation

☐ Private practice
☐ Local authority
☐ Public/Government department
☐ Contractor
☐ Industrial/Commercial company
☐ Research establishment
☐ College/University (*state below*)
☐ Other (*state below*)

ARCHITECTURAL DESIGN

☐ I wish to subscribe to *Architectural Design* at the full rate
☐ I wish to subscribe to *Architectural Design* at the student rate
☐ I wish to subscribe for a friend to *Architectural Design* at the full rate
☐ I wish to subscribe for a friend to *Architectural Design* at the student rate
.... **Starting date:** ☐ From issue 1/2/98
            ☐ From next available issue

.... **Payment enclosed by Cheque/ Money Order/ Drafts**
    Value/Currency £/US$...
.... **Please charge £/US$.........................to my credit card**

Account no:

Expiry date:

Card: Visa/Amex/Mastercard/Eurocard (*delete as applicable*)

Cardholder's signature...
Cardholder's name...
Address...
....**Post/Zip Code:**........................

Recipient's name..
Address...
....**Post/Zip Code:**........................

Please indicate your job title

☐ Architect
☐ Landscape Architect
☐ Architectural Technician/Assistant
☐ Surveyor
☐ Building Services Engineer
☐ Town Planner
☐ Interior Designer
☐ Designer
☐ Building Contractor
☐ Property Developer
☐ Student (*state college/university below*)
☐ Other (*state below*)

Please indicate your organisation

☐ Private practice
☐ Local authority
☐ Public/Government department
☐ Contractor
☐ Industrial/Commercial company
☐ Research establishment
☐ College/University (*state below*)
☐ Other (*state below*)

ARCHITECTURAL DESIGN

☐ I wish to subscribe to *Architectural Design* at the full rate
☐ I wish to subscribe to *Architectural Design* at the student rate
☐ I wish to subscribe for a friend to *Architectural Design* at the full rate
☐ I wish to subscribe for a friend to *Architectural Design* at the student rate
.... **Starting date:** ☐ From issue 1/2/98
            ☐ From next available issue

.... **Payment enclosed by Cheque/ Money Order/ Drafts**
    Value/Currency £/US$...
.... **Please charge £/US$.........................to my credit card**

Account no:

Expiry date:

Card: Visa/Amex/Mastercard/Eurocard (*delete as applicable*)

Cardholder's signature...
Cardholder's name...
Address...
....**Post/Zip Code:**........................

Recipient's name..
Address...
....**Post/Zip Code:**........................

Please indicate your job title

☐ Architect
☐ Landscape Architect
☐ Architectural Technician/Assistant
☐ Surveyor
☐ Building Services Engineer
☐ Town Planner
☐ Interior Designer
☐ Designer
☐ Building Contractor
☐ Property Developer
☐ Student (*state college/university below*)
☐ Other (*state below*)

Please indicate your organisation

☐ Private practice
☐ Local authority
☐ Public/Government department
☐ Contractor
☐ Industrial/Commercial company
☐ Research establishment
☐ College/University (*state below*)
☐ Other (*state below*)

Architectural Design

EPHEMERAL/PORTABLE
ARCHITECTURE

OPPOSITE: YNGVE BERGQUIST, ÅKE LARSSON AND KAKO NORDSTRÖM, JUKKASJÄRVI ICE HOTEL, SWEDEN
ABOVE: BRANSON COATES ARCHITECTURE, POWERHOUSE::UK, HORSE GUARD'S PARADE, LONDON

ACADEMY EDITIONS • LONDON

Acknowledgements

We would like to express our gratitude to all the contributors to *Architectural Design* and in particular to Robert Kronenburg for guest-editing this issue.

All material is courtesy of the authors and architects unless otherwise stated. Attempts have been made to locate the sources of all photographs to obtain full reproduction rights, but in the very few cases where this process has failed to find the copyright holder, our apologies are offered. Photographic credits: *p1* Vladimir Krstic; *p3* Philip Vine; *p8 left* Shelter Publications Ltd; *pp2, 17, 19-20* Camilla Wirseen; *p30 below* Jennifer Krogh; *p37 above and below* Derk Jan Wooldrik; *p53* Tomio Ohashi; *pp61-68, 69 above* Michael Reisch; *p92* Phil Sayer

Front Cover: Computer-generated image from Lena Nalbach, Horse, 1996
Inside Covers: Günter Zamp Kelp, model of *Jahrtausendblick*, Millennium View Stonesigns, Steinbergen, Germany

EDITOR: Maggie Toy
DEPUTY EDITOR: Ellie Duffy
DESIGN: Mario Bettella and Andrea Bettella/Artmedia

First published in Great Britain in 1998 by *Architectural Design*
42 LEINSTER GARDENS, LONDON W2 3AN

A division of John Wiley & Sons
Baffins Lane, Chichester, West Sussex PO19 1UD

ISBN: 0-471-98422-1

Printed and bound in Italy

Contents

ARCHITECTURAL DESIGN PROFILE No 135
EPHEMERAL/PORTABLE ARCHITECTURE
Guest-edited by Robert Kronenburg

Yngve Bergquist, Åke Larsson and Kako Nordström, Jukkasjärvi Ice Hotel, Sweden, computer rendering of interior

ROBERT KRONENBURG
EPHEMERAL ARCHITECTURE

The way in which you are and I am, the way in which we humans are on the earth, is dwelling . . .

Martin Heidegger[1]

An accurate definition of the ephemeral is that which lasts for just one day – more commonly we think of ephemeral experiences as transitory ones, though of indeterminate length. It is almost automatic to assume that such fleeting experiences are relatively inconsequential. However, though they may be temporary in duration, their impact can be lasting: the fleeting memory from childhood may become an individual's most potent recollection and its power be such that it helps focus, or destroy, an entire life. It is therefore the power of the experience rather than its duration that is more important in gauging its meaning and effect.

Heidegger believed that anywhere on the earth and under the sky became our dwelling once we became capable of dwelling – the whole of the world became part of our 'inside' space; dwelling did not need buildings to take place. Although the need for architecture springs from the pragmatic need for shelter, once this function has been fulfilled the role of architecture then serves other purposes such as identifying place, belonging and ownership. It is 'dwelling' in this sense to which Heidegger refers. These purposes are concerned with the spiritual part of life rather than the physical and are recognised by the mind and recalled in its memory.

In terms of architecture, even the most ephemeral structure has the power to form a sign that we identify as 'place', which in turn is linked intricately with other powerful concepts of occupation and definitions of territory. As temporary structures were the first forms of architecture to be erected, they have the potential to make a direct connection with every person's ability to make architecture in a way that more complex forms cannot. They also therefore have the power to encapsulate, in the most immediate way, the primal act of building.

The experience of making and remaking architecture is significant, both for those involved and for those watching the process. The erection of a building that takes place over a comfortable attention time-span has more power to be retained in the memory as an event. Temporary structures, built quickly and in connection with a specific occasion, have this intrinsic connection with the establishment of event phenomena, for they tap into essential 'of the day' ephemeral qualities. Such structures appear to have a latent energy encoded within their fabric – when dissembled there is the potential for erection into a usable form; when in use, there is the knowledge that one day soon they may be taken apart.

Portable architecture, made to be erected repetitively, uses forms of construction that are linked most intimately with its essence – in many cases its form is therefore expressive of its structural system, materiality and erection process. It can be

argued convincingly that the form and character of these buildings are therefore easier to read for those involved in their operation and use.

The possibility of deconstruction (destruction!), which is inherent in all architecture, inevitably affects the notion of its creation, its use, and the knowledge that eventually it will, in time, fall into disuse. Buildings remain in use because of dedicated acts towards their maintenance and operation. If this system fails or is ignored the building fabric will suffer, eventually beyond effective repair. Unlike the normal course of events in nature, which is self-regenerating, architecture requires direct human action to ensure its continuity. Portable buildings can be perceived as relating more to the cyclic quality of life, for in their destruction lies their ultimate rebirth – the ebb and flow of construction/ destruction, the cycle of 'building/building-in-use/dismantling' reflects the growth/death cycle found in the living world.

The ephemeral qualities that are most easily observed in portable building also have value in buildings meant for continuous use on more permanent sites. These qualities may be utilised in static architecture in order to make it more immediate, more understandable, and more recognisable, and to help accentuate demarcations of place and space for building users. The notion of event in architecture is one which can also be appropriated by architects designing buildings for more permanent functions on a specific site, so that the individual will take note of time and event in their use of the building in ways that allude to the cycle of the day, the seasons, patterns of building use and life. The sensitivity to delicacy and economy of structure and form found in the best lightweight transportable architecture is a valuable tool in expressing the form of any building and the relationship between its space-making and space-generation qualities.

The essays and projects collected together in this issue of *Architectural Design* explore the characteristics of the temporary and tenuous in architecture. A critical feature of this collection is that the ephemeral has as important a place in the 'permanent' structures, which have been designed to relate to well-defined functions on a specific location, as it does in the temporary buildings, designed either for a limited time and purpose or for use in a variety of sites. This issue is therefore not just about portable architecture, but about the ephemeral qualities that can be recognised and are of value in all forms of architecture.

Vladimir Krstic's essay makes it clear that transient and transportable notions of architecture are at the root of traditional Japanese constructional form, and that these notions continue to have a profound effect in the establishment of the relevance and continuity of architecture today through the work of contemporary architects like Toyo Ito. Perhaps even more fundamentally, the ideas put forward in his essay suggest that the simplest of human actions establish the foundations for the generation of architectural form, and those actions should be recognised and maintained in order to ensure historical and cultural continuity.

Katsura Villa, Kyoto

VLADIMIR KRSTIC

CONSTRUCTING THE EPHEMERAL

The Notions of Binding and Portability in Japanese Architecture

Although ephemerality could be seen primarily as a conceptual architectural proposition, the condition of being ephemeral resides in the technique of construction and the concept of materiality that is embedded in it.

In Japanese Shinto rites, the act of tying a rope – the sacred rope *Shimenawa* – around an object or a place demarcates a location at which a divine spirit (*Kami*) will descend and temporarily inhabit the world of the living. The tying, or more precisely the act of binding, embodies simultaneously a couple of different conceptual notions: it inscribes and creates the territory, implies its occupation, and generates meaning by signifying the existence of the sacred spirit.

The Japanese word *Shime* (verb *shime-ru*: to close [tie]) from which the word *Shimenawa* (the tying [sacred] rope) is inferred has, according to Günter Nitschke, its etymological roots in three words: 'a) *Shimeru* (Old Japanese: *Shimaru*) – to bind, to close, to sum up; b) *Shimeru* (Old Japanese: *Shimu*) – to occupy; c) *Shimesu* (Old Japanese: same) – to signify.'[1] He further asserts, following the premise of ergological etymology, according to which objects in archaic times were named after the way in which they were made, that the idea of *Shime* denotes a cosmogonic structure whose meaning originates in the process of its making: 'What was made was a *bound* (a) artifact which *signified* (b) an *occupation* (c) of land. What was made was a *Shime*; and in ancient and in modern Japanese, up to recent times, that was exactly the term for an occupation mark. In our opinion it could only receive this name from the way it was made, namely by binding.'[2]

Hence the act of binding denotes an archetypal mode of construction, an instance of willed human action by way of which an undifferentiated natural condition is transformed into a state of cosmogonic order. Furthermore, it could be argued that binding understood as a construction constitutes a primordial act of making architecture which, informed by and born out of a very specific idea of cosmogony, inscribes a peculiar form of architectural conceptualisation.

In order to further explore architecture that is analogous with the idea of *Shime* it is necessary to consider the concepts that underlie the act of binding. According to the cosmogonic view of Shinto religion, the gods (*Kami* – divine [ancestral] spirits) reside in the invisible and inaccessible depths of the sea or the mountains and they manifest themselves only for a brief period of time when they, on a cyclical time basis, come to visit particular locations in the world of the living. The tying of the sacred rope *Shimenawa* not only inscribes the territory and signifies its occupation (by a divine spirit) but, more importantly, it denotes the impermanence of the event that takes place within the inscribed territory – in Shinto terminology *Yori-shiro*, or a temporary divine visiting place. The temporariness here appears as a double 'theme' of the construction technique. On the one hand, the purpose of the construction is to signify and allow for the temporariness (of the event of divine appearance) to be materialised through the symbolic function of its structure. On the other hand, the construction itself, having its origin in the signification of the temporariness, is conceived as a physical analogue of that which it signifies and is executed as a temporary thing, whether in regard to the technique (being demountable [untied]), materiality (rope, grass and other perishable natural materials), or destructibility (propensity for burning in straw). Ultimately, it could be argued that the purpose of the act of binding a sacred rope is to construct temporariness.

The constructed temporariness incorporates two permanent elements that partake in its making (it actually unfolds as a function of their mutual relation): the place and the construction technique. The place constitutes a constant in terms of its idea, or the ideology of seeing that informs its discrimination, a characteristic natural condition sought out and received as a potential (an idiosyncratic configuration of an animate or inanimate object, or a locale, like a tree trunk or a rock that in its extraordinariness bears a sign of divinity and has a capacity to be inhabited by the divine spirit), which invites perpetual acts of construction. The place, its permanence, is consequently recognised more in terms of latent capacities rather than as an actuality. It is solely through the mediation of the 'construction', the tying of the rope, that the place is truly actualised, though, as discussed above, only on a temporary basis.

Parallel to this peculiar idea of the permanence of place, the construction technique – the tying of the rope – emerges as a second constant. It is conceived as such solely in terms of the precision and the exactness of the binding method, which in the fixity of its principle transcends all circumstantial conditions, including topological idiosyncrasies, and imposes itself in a form of applied universality through its construction technique. So the impermanence here appears in the difference of the constancy of the method of 'reading' of a place and the constancy of the application of the 'science' of a universalised construction method.

Herein lies the particular architectural epitome: on the one hand, the place and placing of architecture is conceived as a critical reference point, but only in a temporary sense as a location within which an architectural construction unfolds (in terms of demarcation, occupation and signification) strictly for a limited period of time. On the other hand, the technique and the means of the construction of architecture are divorced entirely from the conditions of any individual place. They are never site-specific and embody the minimum necessary elements (the binding of a rope) that allow an architectural structure to produce its meaning-generation effect in all conceivable locations.

Hence the idea of portability emerges as an arguable constituting element of the archetypal condition of Japanese architecture. This idea, however, does not inscribe a literal condition of architecture as being necessarily physically portable (although that always remains an open and inherent possibility); rather, it denotes a conceptual notion that informs the process

Shimogamo Shrine, Kyoto

Kuramara Mountain Shrine

Gion Festival float construction, Kyoto

of the phenomenal constitution of an architectural object.

A number of points demonstrate the analogies between the concept of *Shime* and the archetypal idea of Japanese architecture. Probably the most relevant of these is the notion of 'Shared Space' proposed by Mitsuo Inoue.[3] According to him the interior space in Japanese architecture was conceived traditionally as a realm, not only reserved for and occupied by humans, but also deities and ancestral spirits. (Their existence was acknowledged in annual rituals through the demarcation of the physical invisibility of a sacred spirit.) In this respect, the house represents a sacred as much as a secular structure.

Consequently, the act of making architecture could be regarded as a conceptual parallel of the process of demarcation, occupation and signification found in the practice of *Shimenawa*, since it in part fulfils the same purpose of inscribing the ground (creating the world) where the sacred spirit can manifest itself. Moreover, it could be argued that the traditional post and beam structure with the pronounced absence of walls, bears, in material and physical sense, conceptual semblance to the effect of the binding of a rope: as in *Shimenawa* the resulting structure is physically minimal and remains permeable. Its purpose is not to hold within, by enclosing and disconnecting, but by signifying and demarcating, whereby creation of an opaque architectural structure is rendered inconceivable. The motive of the construction process appears to be a pursuit of physical dissolution, a continuous attempt and a desire to unmake architecture in its physical presentness in order to exchange it for and replace it with its experiential effects. To that extent architecture is realised as a tenuous entity – a transparent frame and a shadowy stage-ground wherein the transience of things (deities) and events is seduced into marking its passage.

The site itself, however, is actually signified and created through architectural construction. Architecture conceived as a frame, an instrument of signification that operates through topological demarcation, allows for that which is inherent and latent in a particular location to disclose itself, or make the idea of itself tangible. It binds the site into being by giving measure to the intangibility of things that underlie it – the site is made real in reference to that which is thought to reside in it, literally in the depths of the ground.[4]

Yet, paradoxically, it is the location (place) that endures rather than architecture. The Japanese are very reluctant to give up a piece of land but they have very little concern for the eventual removal of an architectural structure that might be sitting on it. This can be understood hypothetically as a further indication of the conceptual analogy that exists between acts of tying (*Shimenawa*) and constructing (architecture). In the most abstract conceptual terms, both of these constructs perform an identical function and have identical meaning relative to the idea of site. They are signs (its denotative structures), and as such are identical and qualitatively indistinguishable from each other, and thus exchangeable.

There appears to be no conceptual difference between the binding of a sacred rope and constructing a building on a particular site with regard to the meaning they produce. Since their purpose resides in the interposing function of a sign, their material permanence is of little relevance. They are materially neither grounded in the duration of time nor the persistence of their objecthood, but in the state of their own presentness – they simply are, in an atemporal (temporary) fashion, by being signs of that which is physically invisible. Consequently, in spite of their physical difference, architecture is not perceived to be any more permanent than a simple structure of a bound (sacred) rope. What remains constant is the idea of place, pregnant with its indiscernible spiritual depths, against which architecture is measured as a transient sign (or the sign of transience).

The phenomenon of temporality around which Japanese traditional architecture is constituted is inseparable from the conceptualisation of the structural assembly of its body. The idea of impermanence in this instance is embedded in the notion of construction technique. In other words, the part of the physical make-up of something that is temporary is a dimension and a potential for its own undoing, it actually represents its defining characteristic. Traditionally, the connections between major structural elements, beams and post in Japanese architecture were executed through tensile and pressure joints without the use of nails. When necessary, wood pegs and wedges were used to secure connections and the proper distribution of forces.

It could be argued that such a conceptualisation of the structural assembly has its origin in the pragmatics of the earthquake-prone conditions of Japan, where flexible joints would allow for maximum resistance, or, in the case of collapse, preservation of structural elements. Nevertheless, seen from another perspective, it could also be postulated that the idea of

Royanaji Temple, Kyoto   *Daikokuji Temple, Kyoto*

binding (*Shime*) conceptually underlies such a construction method. The idea of binding implies a notion that something is put together by a knot(s) tied around it. As a result of this method, the constitutive elements of a constructed assembly are never altered in their original forms: they are simply brought together by the mediation of a rope. Therefore, any such produced structure is always provisional rather then absolute. More importantly, tying (the making of a knot) denotes and opens up the possibility of its own unmaking (untying) without material destruction and alteration of either binding or bound material. Here resides a critical distinction of binding and building, or understanding a particular form of construction as binding. Whatever is bound is only temporary until it fulfils its function, whereupon it can be unbound, disassembled and erased, or made (bound) into something else.

It is not only *Shimenawa* that is removed after the deity is gone, quite often traditional houses in Japan are moved from one location to another by being disassembled and assembled systematically. This suggests an understanding of architecture as a system of abstractly universal structural and meaning-generating elements which are in flux and dependent upon the precision of the assembly principle to produce their effect. It is within this conceptual framework that the idea of portability in Japanese architecture resides.

Phenomenally, in the context of the idea of *Shime* as its underlying conceptual referent, Japanese traditional architecture has been constituted into a paradoxical structure. The notion of architecture as an analogue of the 'bound artifact which signifies the occupation of land' can not be separated from the phenomenal nature of that which such an artifact is supposed to signify. The material origin of architecture resides in the fact that the act of binding, framing through construction, is supposed to bring within the realm of the visible something that by its nature is invisible – the sacred spirit that has no anthropomorphic configuration. Consequently, the whole building process unfolds as a speculative undertaking of making a stage, inscribing a territory, wherein the invisible will manifest itself.

The paradox of this situation resides in the fact that in attempting to bring forth something that exists outside the spectrum of the real (visible), and in doing so becoming an instrument of its disclosure, architecture itself has grown more indeterminable in its presence and material veracity. In other words, architecture has come to approximate in its own physical make-up the character of that which it was trying to contain. Ultimately, architecture is resolved into a state in which the stage could not be separated from the event, where matter dissolves into shadow and the movement of air into anticipation of something happening; a place where there is no known form to things and where time translates into apprehension; a moment when something fleeting is caught by the corner of the eye. The material reality of architecture in Japanese tradition is, hence, conceived only in relative terms, as a counter-instance, but not more relevant, to that which is absent of matter; its body circumscribes a place of intersection and exchange between the real and the unreal and is literally made out of it – the tenuous construction of transience (*Shimenawa*).

The question remains to what extent the aforementioned ideas of conceptual and material configurations of architecture are relevant today, when the terms of architectural practice, production and ideology have changed drastically. If it is understood that these ideas are grounded in a particular world-view and denote a specific sensibility for apprehending and relating to the larger order circumstances, then it could be argued that the resulting architectural archetype has preserved its relevance as a matrix for the reconstitution of architecture's material and conceptual bearings.

The idea of temporariness started, curiously, to (re)emerge in the mid 80s in the works and writings of the contemporary Japanese architect Toyo Ito and has continued to carry on into the present. This way of thinking has taken place at a critical juncture for Japanese architects, with the painfully tangible realisation of the futility of extending the ideology of the 'Urban Guerrilla' (propagated by Tadao Ando). Its promise of a prolonged stand-off situation between architecture and the city was threatening, with the conceptual cul-de-sac of architecture once again becoming its own purpose. In refocusing the question of the city and reinterpreting it as a metaphor of Nature – 'The Urban Forest' as a man-made technological Nature – Ito was able to reframe his own architectural explorations conceptually. The city was no longer a condition and a context to be resisted; rather, it was accepted in its inevitable 'natural' presence as a place of architecture. As such, it circumscribed the ground on which architecture had to be reconfigured conceptually and materially in order to come to terms with the ideological shift in its contextual parameters; the idea of 'second' nature and the

LEFT: Toyo Ito, T Building, Tokyo, 1990; RIGHT, FROM ABOVE: Toyo Ito, Silver Hut, Tokyo, 1984; Toyo Ito, Ueda Gallery, Tokyo, 1991

'naturalness' of technology and electronics in constituting the body of the city. Ito himself wrote:

> Architecture has always had an existence easily visible by architects. However, if the forest we are currently living in is an invisible space and houses we are dwelling in cannot be clearly objectivised, we are destined to be thrown out again into the wild forests and fields which are cities.[5]

Analogously, the idea of 'primitive' architecture (hut) has surfaced here as the next logical question and the matrix for the new way of thinking.

Ito approached the idea of primitive architecture in terms of the reductive essence of an architectural structure; the state in which what is constructed and conceived bears no material difference to its context, the only distinction being the deliberate manner of organising (assembling) the material in order to produce a meaning-generating condition. The paradigm delineated by this question has implied consideration of two parallel conditions. On the one hand, architecture had to dispense with the protective formal shell embedded in its ordering systems to make a liberating recourse in confronting the issue of its origin. On the other hand, the metaphorical idea of 'nature' was based in an understanding of technology, the high technology of electronics, as a new fibre which was necessitating material and conceptual reconstitution of architecture and, at the same time, allowing for the question of the 'primitive' to be framed anew. Together with this, the city as a 'forest' was understood, analogous to Abbé Laugier's idea, as a repository of building material from where, or from whose technological body, architecture was to be gathered.

What is of interest to this argument is the fact that the concept of construction of architecture in Ito's work incarnates notions of territorial demarcation and signification of occupation reflective of the idea of *Shime*. One could postulate that the essence of Ito's architecture resides in the study of matter. The form never exists outside of the realm of material that produces it and, in a certain sense, it is the material that dominates form and renders it abstract. However, that dominance is not contained in the tangibility of the presence of the material but in the art of transforming it into an ephemeral state in which it is revealed as its own negation: it neither is, nor it is not. The walls in Ito's architecture are painstakingly-constructed, feeble structures whose permeable substance lack the capacity to either hold things or to keep them out – it is the event of the transmission of things through their substance that makes them real.

Similar to the act of binding a sacred rope, the meaning of architecture is revealed in the demarcation of the transparency of its locus. It is made by that which fleetingly transpires and leaves its quickly fading residue in the folds of the building matter. Ito himself has argued that:

> architecture is an extremely transient existence like a piece of film wrapping a human body. It does not have a substance nor implies weight. Designing an architecture is an

act of generating vortexes in the currents of air, wind, light and sound. It is not constructing a dam against flow nor resigning oneself to the current.[6]

The attempt to construct transience, to make a stage for something temporary to unfold in this case, is not based in the quest for the revelation of a divine presence, it seeks something equally elusive and invisible – the etherealised effects of technology and nature. However, what matters here is the idea of anticipation: the desiring and sensing of that which is not defined in advance and has no known form, nor is measurable. This is what connects Ito's work, in spirit and sensibility, with the tradition of Japanese architecture, and the idea of *Shime*.

The idea of transience in his work extends beyond phenomenal configurations of architecture and carries over into larger questions of sociopolitical conscience of architectural production which stem from his contemplation of the condition of Japanese city. This, in the first place, relates to the concept of 'urban nomad' as a fictitious and archetypal inhabitant of Ito's work. The concept implies the condition of placelessness and the life of wandering to which the inhabitants of contemporary metropolis are subjugated today. The corollary of this situation is the loss of place of architecture, or the problematisation of the idea of fixed site. What is postulated here is not the idea of the doom of sitelessness, but rather the notion of architecture sited in the city (its condition), as a whole where individual physical place becomes a thing of a lesser consequence for the construction of architecture.

Such a realisation, though still hypothetical, resonates tangibly in the manner in which Ito's buildings have been put together. They appear to be connected to the site only tenuously. The air caught in the strained concaves of the vaulted roof shells gives a stronger sense of grounding to the buildings than the soil itself, creating a sense of an architecture that virtually glides in the place. Simultaneously, the very idiosyncrasy of the formal topography of these structures inscribes its own uncertainty – the form occurs as an almost circumstantial configuration of the prefabricated structural system that underlies it. Within the outline of the prefabricated body of the form-generating skeleton lurks the possibility of continuous and boundless transformation: a chance for undoing and reassembling, making anew and moving to another place where form materialises only as an interlude between two states of transformation. And no matter what kind of transformation, the material always remains unaltered: an instrument of open possibilities of construction, of making of the world irrespective of location. This is where the idea of making in Ito's architecture becomes analogous to the binding of a sacred rope, and this is where the circle is completed, or started anew.

This essay is based on a paper presented to the first international conference on portable architecture, held in London in May 1997, the proceedings of which are to be published in Transportable Environments *by E & FN Spon (London) in late 1998*

Notes

1 Günter Nitschke, 'Shime, Binding/Unbinding', *Architectural Design* 12, 1974.
2 Ibid.
3 Mitsuo Inoue, *Space in Japanese Architecture*, Weatherhill (New York), 1985.
4 Most of the new building construction in Japan is preceded by the 'Tokoro

Shizume Matsuri', the Land Quietening Ritual, the purpose of which is to seek redemption with the residing deities for disturbing the land.
5 Toyo Ito, 'Architecture Sought After by Android', *Japan Architect* 06/1988.
6 Toyo Ito, 'Vortex and Current – An Architecture of Phenomenalism'.

HENRIETTA PALMER
THE AESTHETICS OF DISAPPEARANCE

When Yves Klein was experimenting with air, fire and water in the late 50s, he was obsessed with the idea of sculpturing space with disappearing materials. In his famous act of trading the gallery void for gold leaves and then throwing the leaves into the River Seine, he celebrated the transition of nothingness to value and of value wasted and dissolved in a most sophisticated way.

Ice placed in a warmer temperature alludes to that fascination – the euphoria of disappearance, which in the end is related not to destruction but to creation. A car exposition might be the right place for an awakening of this sensation, challenging the valuable with the presence of dissolution. The SAAB exhibition stand at the Auto Motor Show Geneva in March 1998, by Anders Wilhelmson Architects and Designers, was an investigation of this theme. There they placed a 3 x 12 metre block of ice to melt away among the exposed car models. The precise appearance of their elegant glass construction confronting the equally minimalist but 'alive' block of ice, was a stunning experience for the visitors who approached to touch the slowly vanishing object. Solid ice melting in the warm air does not express the laconic acceptance of entropy, but rather the fundamental joy of recreation.

Even in a harsh Arctic climate, spring eventually returns and defeats constructions of ice and snow. Every year, 2.5 million Swedish Kroner melt away in Jukkasjärvi in the north of Sweden, where 4,000 square metres of snow buildings – hotel, chapel and exhibition halls – are erected yearly. 'It's the relief of the disappearance that triggers the creativity of the next year's construction,' explains Yngve Bergquist, who is responsible for the Jukkasjärvi Ice Hotel. Snow and ice architecture, once an everyday reality for Inuit people, is experiencing a renaissance as a tourist attraction in the Arctic regions of Sweden, Finland and Japan. As such, it fulfils the demands of this modern pilgrimage.

In the words of architect Eija Antilla, designer of the third annual Snow Castle in the Finnish town Kemi – a two-storey-high snow construction and the largest in the world – the 'unreality' and the childlike attributes of the apparently innocent, pure whiteness, recall fairy-tale memories and establish a dream world suitable for the get-away-from-the-ordinary magic of tourism. But one can also claim that the physically extreme condition of such cold temperatures awakens the marvel of the imagined 'real life' of those once living day-to-day in snow architecture (according to sociological studies, 'real life acting' is now a tourist attraction as 'simple' living has become unobtainable by Western tourists). However, the most important quality that transforms snow architecture into an event, mentally and physically, and encourages visitors to return for new experiences, is the knowledge of its ultimate dissolution.

  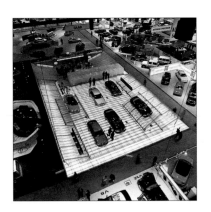

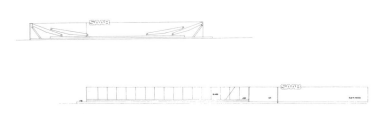

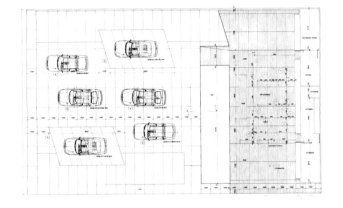

Anders Wilhelmson Architects and Designers/collaborator Marina Karlman, SAAB Showcase, Auto Motor Show, Geneva 1998; BELOW: Plan and elevations; OPPOSITE: Yngve Bergquist, Åke Larsson and Kako Nordström, Jukkasjärvi Ice Hotel, Sweden

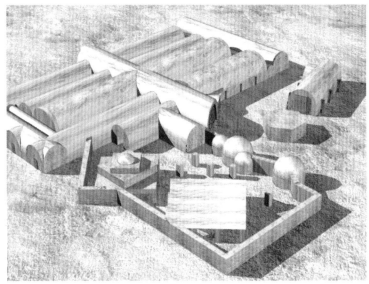

Yngve Bergquist, Åke Larsson and Kako Nordström, Jukkasjärvi Ice Hotel, Sweden;
ABOVE: Computer renderings; OPPOSITE: Interior of chapel

In 1997, the Finnish architect Kimmo Kuismanen, who has years of experience of the implications of Arctic conditions on architecture and city planning and has an interest in ecological materials, established the firm SnowHow Ltd with the engineer Seppo Mäkinen. Their objective was to investigate the architectural qualities and possibilities of construction using ice and snow. Mäkinen developed computer programs for snow engineering which explored the strength and behaviour of snow as a building material. In Snow Town Aurora 1997-98, an 'event-city' next to the Finlandia house in Helsinki, SnowHow Ltd explored the plastic qualities of snow in 10-metre-tall cone shaped restaurant structures. 'Ice architecture tends to be banal,' explains Kuismanen, 'exploiting traditional crafts and geometries to become kitsch rather than new architecture. Our aim is to bring building art to snow building.'

In Jukkasjärvi, as well as in Kemi, the construction method has been developed over years (patented by Kako Nordström) and based on moulding principles rather than the traditional igloo block building. Artificial snow is shot on to steel moulds to shape 'vaults'. The snow sets for two or three days before the mould is moved to an adjacent position to repeat the process – creating, in the end, a tunnel space. To prevent the vaults from sagging, ice columns drilled in segments out of the Torne River ice are stacked in the middle of the space. 'The wet snow is a tenacious material. Think of it as textile,' says the Stockholm architect Love Arbén in relation to the seemingly awkward position of the ice columns which support the roof of his Ice Exhibition Pavilion, erected in central Stockholm as part of the Cultural Capital of Europe celebrations in 1998. The snow vaults are more akin to a tent than a masonry construction – the columns working as tent poles, tightening the 'soft' material.

The Stockholm Pavilion was built with a refrigerating system installed into the walls and floors in order to avoid the physical effects caused by a mild climate. The problem of making artificial snow in warmer temperatures was solved by using leftover snow from ice-skating rinks. 'An ecological use of a material otherwise thrown away,' explains Bergquist, who was also in charge of the construction of the Stockholm Pavilion. 'But our next constructive and architectural challenge,' he continues, 'will be pure ice masonry.' It is the ice itself that is so marvellous, drawing the light into the snow-enclosed spaces and catching the colour of the sky even on a grey day. The transparent river ice, shimmering in turquoise, is completely in tune with the pervasive minimalist outlook. It is no wonder that the Swedish car industry, striving to communicate high quality and elegance, was immediately attracted to the appearance of the ice block melting on the glass floor.

Snow architecture is an interior experience, the exterior being difficult to control as a result of constant weathering. An amorphous mound hides a defined concavity, an imprint. To a greater extent than any other architecture, the snow space involves the human body. The cold keeps the body moving, thereby establishing an architecture that contradicts itself in terms of what architecture is, through the creation of a place that is impossible for dwelling or resting. The Inuits warmed their small igloos with the heat of their bodies, reaching temperatures of +15°C. However, in the spacious halls of Jukkasjärvi Ice Hotel the temperature stays at five degrees below, unaffected by the visitors. In previous years an ice sauna has been built in Jukkas, with temperatures reaching +40°C. The physical sensation of a naked body against a bench of ice brings valuable surreal qualities to architecture, which surrenders too easily to a simple iconography.

Back in 1967 Allan Kaprow, father of 'the happening', erected 20 small ice-block buildings during a single day in the Californian town of Pasadena. These structures, which were 10 feet wide, 30 feet long and 8 feet high, without doors or windows, were just left to melt away. The poetics of the disappearing material extended the lifetime of his 'Fluids'. Derived from the happenings of the 60s, the event-industry of tourist attractions is perhaps affecting the permanence of architecture. In this case, ice architecture is the event-architecture, where, in reality, time or no-time, becomes the building material itself.

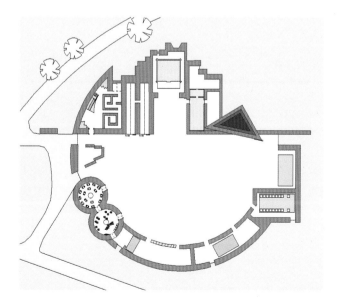 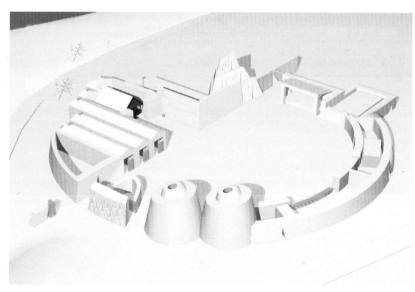

OPPOSITE: Yngve Bergquist, Åke Larsson and Kako Nordström, Jukkasjärvi Ice Hotel, Sweden; ABOVE, L TO R: SnowHow Ltd, Snow Town Aurora, Helsinki 1997-98, plan; axonometric

LEFT: Vincent Golding & Azlina Raja Azwa, Fire Tower and Stair Platform, 1998, detail; ABOVE: Tom Raymond, Parliament Tent, 1997; BELOW, L TO R: Henry Frankish, Flat Pack Dreadnought, 1992; Sang Il Hoon, Rabbit Chariot, 1997

MARK PRIZEMAN

INTENSITY

Portable Architecture as Parable

Looking down upon the face of the earth, it is only the remains of fixed buildings that survive to tell us of a society's aims. The only physical evidence of the transient and mobile societies are the paths, no different from the tracks of wild animals, that move from one hunting ground to another littered with scattered broken artifacts.

Today this transient architecture continues and the physical evidence is all too easily misunderstood. Like a bicycle pulled from a canal, merely a relic minus a few essential components, it is the act of moving that makes it understandable. The problem with describing portable architecture – be it a fireworks display, rock concert or the army of Genghis Khan – is that no part stays still at the same time as another. The whole edifice is never there long enough to be complete and it is the relationship of one space to another that has to be understood, after all.

It is in the transition from hunter gatherer to farmer that the origins of architecture are based. The remnants of the nomadic soul are the basic language of the historical forms of architecture. The bound reeds and vegetative decoration that are the coded ingredients of Ancient Egyptian, Mesopotamian, Mayan, Chinese, Greek, or whatever, telling us a cogent hierarchical story. Perhaps a clearer way of understanding the power of architecture is to start with the nomad placing portable structures in a variety of special places with due regard to the context and climate – the ability to adapt and lead one's life free from the requirement to leave physical evidence of it.

Nomads in their wanderings over the face of the earth consider the landscape as common territory and do not seek to leave their mark upon its face. The essentially all-pervading nature of the nomad's life (Berbers, gypsies, travellers, etc) that so annoys current governments is the same gadfly that so upset the ancient Greeks and their concept of citizenship. The restless urge to wander over the face of the Earth through an ever changing scenery, without altering it or possessing it, is anathema to the prescribed rules of civilisation. The punishment of landscape by architecture is as old as Ozymandias, but the nomad accommodates the natural features of mountains and streams in architecture, noting their relative placement and imbuing them with cosmic powers, much as the rooms in a temple. The ability to disappear and leave no trace is a common theme and one which volume house builders should be reminded of. But then real architecture nowadays is to do with having a fashionable sense of soul, or is it style?

The direct link from the nomad's yurt to Modernism is by way of Le Corbusier. His direct observations in his 'Journey to the East ' are poignant: on seeing the Turkish houses stacked up the hills in Bosnia and Constantinople he conceived the tower block. The traditional Turkish house consists of a number of self-contained square rooms (*Odas*) which are derived generically and functionally from the open-plan yurt, organised around an open area (*Sofa*) which links the *Odas*. The arrangement of the

houses up the hills allows a sense of privacy, while providing each house with a clear view over the neighbouring dwellings. If you imagine this stacked situation with the hill removed you are left with the Unité de Habitation.

The Tent Project, run by First Year Unit 3 at the Architectural Association in London for the past 11 years, has a variety of ancestors, living relations and disparate offspring. It was started in 1987 as a response to the then First Year Technical Study requirement for students to execute in the AA workshop a full-size detail of one of their designs for a building. The concept was to both introduce students to an understanding of the physical craft involved in architecture and illustrate that the detail of a building could contain the ethos of the whole.

The Tent Project takes the idea further by constructing a complete building: an individual's first building that has to perform within a group, the ethos of the whole then being truly reflected in the details. These details are all connected with the essential requirement of portability. Due to its longevity the project has started to display evidence of evolution and divergence. To spend a cold night in a futuristic structure made using essentially Medieval methods of construction is a test of the integrity of the design to reach a satisfactory resolution. Eleven years later the project has evolved within the changing academic context of the AA; the argument between whether a drawing is derived from the object or whether it is the drawing that should determine the result.

Conventionally, architects are taught that what they draw is what will happen. This is a very foolish handicap to be blighted with since it leads either to banality or loss of control once something is constructed. The success of a tent depends on the exploration of an idea in the workshop by wandering through the dream and not being restricted by the finite parameters of a drawn representation of the future object. So learning how to control the gestation of an idea by full involvement with its manufacture is achieved by using drawings as calculations. The resolution of the projects in drawn form happens only after the tents have been tested and includes descriptions of the events surrounding this occasion.

The request to spend a night in something that you have made appeals to the primal urge in us to make a house. Moreover, it is not a difficult task to make in a couple of hours something that will keep you warm and dry in inclement weather: tramps, soldiers and hunters all manage quite sufficiently. It is the idea that a combined collection of structures will form a settlement or miniature instant city that provides the inspiration to push the programme further. The tents have to be capable of being transported to a field and erected easily in the cold darkness of the English countryside in mid winter. The Unit is then thrown back on its own resources and demands the mutual cooperation of members to exist. Like explorers planning to venture into the unknown, an ability to imagine the consequences of what one takes and what one leaves behind is imperative.

A budget of £50 to £70 for materials for the Tent Project limits the indulgence of an idea and encourages a hungry eye for the opportune. Methods of construction are not prescribed and new ways are often chanced upon during the construction process, or are developed from the experiences of previous expeditions. Sponsorship, salvage and recycling all play their part. An agenda or manifesto is drawn-up to focus the investigations. New and untested possibilities often arise from the use of unfamiliar combinations of materials. Seminars are given by people working commercially at the forefront of manufacturing skills; for example, furniture makers, fashion designers and alternative research labs.

Making things in an almost Medieval manner and discovering techniques and methods in a hands-on improvisational way is a major design tool. If you do not know exactly how something is to be made intuition needs to be employed, and chance to force progress in realising the structure. A feel for materials and how they misbehave is only learnt by direct experience. The preconceptions of strength and weight become very abstract concepts and are replaced by an attitude of perfecting a method.

The workshop at the AA is equipped with wood and metal working equipment in a room measuring 6 x 20 metres. An enclosed yard suffices for trial erection and other techniques. The structures are then packed into a van and taken on a four-hour journey into the isolated countryside. Dark is usually setting in by the time the various components are unpacked, and the first structures to be assembled are those which have foreseen this occasion and can accommodate extra recumbents.

Each structure has its chosen social function and location within the unit's notional 'instant village'. These are first presented as 1:20 sketch models arranged in an imagined site around a central fire chalked out on the studio floor. In addition to the primal requirement of shelter, each tent had to provide a service for the community as a whole. Each year's selection contains the reworkings of some previous themes of Tower, Observation Platform, Shell Structure, Space Frame, Zoomorphic Shelter and good plain Service to the Community Tent. Eventually, shelter can be challenged. Pontus Brushwitz's 1992 Observation Tower started a cycle of proposals; subsequently also fertilised by the 1994 Machine Project.

In attempting to catalogue the projects we find similarities and affinities of, as yet, untold stories that will need to be with each other on that silent hill witnessing the fall of architecture in the valleys below.

Once on site, the weather and the landscape dominate and it is the responsibility of the group to pitch their structures in a manner that justifies the previous months' effort. By being in the field with the tents, one participates in a performance where everybody thinks that they know their lines and are disparately making others listen. It is the antithesis of suburbanisation, the industrial reconciliation with nature where the rules of civilisation kill what is ugly. For it is in the field that one is literally 'left alone to one's own devices'. When all has passed and these devices are all but destroyed by the passing of time, they are left to inform the next generation with exaggerated tales of success and disaster. Erecting a structure on an isolated hillside and looking out at the twinkling evidence of the rapid descent of England into suburbanisation, one cannot help but think about how this inversion of territory and abuse of landscape has come about and how much one is participating in the situation.

The individual tent is seen only as a fragment, or component within a four-day event which has bound them together to make something else. They are no longer seen as isolated projects, set like advertisements within the beautiful setting. The community formed by the unit on the site is an unpredictable artifact that generates a common experience against which the structure is tested. The structures react and respond to the situation in a spontaneous manner. It is the more successful of these projects that later reflect on this chance collage of dreams on a landscape.

The photographs illustrate this particular moment in the project, that of the improvised setting of a structure against a landscape – as in all the best Westerns where the simple device of setting simple actions against monumental scenery evokes a heroism in even the most trivial domestic scene. It is perhaps part of the lesson that all bad architecture seeks to repress this montage of scales, for it is the simple everyday tasks of shelter and community that these edifices seek to provide. Like the 'benders' being inhabited at the same time 20 or so miles away by the protesters at the bypass, the relatively simple and crude methods of manufacturing could seek to test certain ideas of scale, presence and function in the English landscape.

It is an initial concept that is allowed to dream and grow that can accommodate the details for true portability. A selection of disparate unconnected objects from a museum feeds the initial reaction to the brief, for it is the manner in which something is made, the soul within that needs to be understood. Railway engines, boats and aeroplanes have evolved along similar lines yet their souls are as different as the elements through which they travel. The smoke-box door on a steam train is a facade of cast iron that speaks of the weight of all behind it; the hinges, solid expressive elements. The nose cone of Concorde is a casting of Araldite resin which droops to distinguish itself from other inferior modes of transport. The forming and steaming of green timbers make the hull of a ship of the line resplendent with its decorated stern.

Assembly details are a crucial element in the development of these structures as they should rely only on themselves for the best effect. The experimental 'Wooller' British motorcycle was an attempt to make a motorcycle that did not require any tools to maintain it. Using parts of the initial disassembly as tools for the next stages, speed of assembly, or the performance of assembly, are all considerations come to bear. A nomad uses what is to

ABOVE, L TO R: Takako, Polypropylene Slug, 1996; Lena Nalbach, Horse, 1996; David Lau, Maze, 1998; Yuka Suganami, Lycra Playroom, 1998; CENTRE, L TO R: Paul Mascaro, Gaudí Kitchen; Vincent Golding and Azlina Raja Azwa, Fire Tower and Stair Platform, 1998; Lena Nalbach, Horse, 1996; Vincent Golding and Azlina Raja Azwa, Fire Tower and Stair Platform, 1998; BELOW LEFT: Yoichiro Akiba, Thatched Ropeway, 1998; BACKGROUND: Yuka Suganami, Lycra Playroom, 1998, detail

FROM ABOVE, L TO R: Morten Bille Jorgensen, Steel Cathedral, 1998; Dimitrios Tsigos, Merry Go Round, 1998; Azlina Raja Azwa, Staircase/ Platform, 1998; Il Hoon Roh, Surveillance Centre, 1998; Asaf Mayer, Tensegrity Pod, 1998; Il Hoon Roh, Surveillance Centre, 1998

hand and able to be replaced or adapted, animal and vegetable sources that can be replenished with only the labour of processing (gleaning\refining) as the moderator. Neat, efficient joints that do not leave the maker groping for nuts in wet grass with a torch grace many of the more successful projects.

The loss of control of the destiny of one's work through a compression of time and situation gives all the more credence to how it is recorded. The unexpected failure, loss or damage of a part should encourage improvisation and invention (if only for a decent photograph!). Mapping of the event using symbols to describe change and the passage of time reveals aspects of the community that could have been foreseen; structural failures, convenient improvisations and the contributions of curious visitors staying for a night or two.

After this stage, the question is how to draw up the structures orthogonally and describe the event for the 'folio'. However, the drawings never quite acknowledge the simple poetic reality of things like gaffer tape wrapped wantonly about a sleeping cocoon as a makeshift repair, or the dusting of snow over a stained canvas hammock; but then it is the dream that is being drafted. Drawing what one knows, after the event, is often harder than drawing what one thinks one knows before. However, there are things that only drawings can capture: like the relationship between a group of first-year architectural students on a hillside and the possible futures that could have occurred.

The military establishment, comprising the most technically advanced nomads, is apocryphal in this role, re-inventing and driving forward technology behind a mask of implacable conservatism. Meticulously recording their history in image, symbol and word, the sergeants' and corporals' stripes in the army originate from the award given by the lord of the manor of a pair of cruck frames to build a cottage – the simplest form of shelter recorded on the sleeves of those given a role beyond simple serf.

The requirements of the project have much to do with developing an ability to explore the ramifications of making an idea physical, and potentially functional, in a previously unknown site that by inhabitation becomes extremely well known and tempered. The Object in The Landscape projects often seek to draw some inference from the site as a way of justifying their presence upon the site. This may be indicative of the modern dilemma concerned with context and the acknowledgement of a pre-existing set of architectural rules. It also harks back to the architect's mythical freedom to build and design in isolation, like a pioneer staking his claim in foreign lands. The nomad pitching up takes stock of the context and follows a portable set of rules or traditions. The difference occurs when one is merely the author of a fragment of the perceived whole and is not in such idealised control of the destiny of one's contribution, nor conversant with the improvised etiquette of the society that will use it. Like all real cities, this is perhaps where chance and time are the real planners.

This points to the real difference between architecture and sculpture. The molestation and layering that a work of architecture both performs and withstands is unacceptable to the mind of the sculptor. So the very nature of the tents' failings is their strength: the hidden stories of unfulfilled ambition resulting from lack of time or finance, and the unexpected uses to which the components can be redirected, create a genuine scene upon a site.

The nomad is bound by the seemingly fixed horizon of his tradition and uses invention as a way to survive starvation. Cro-Magnon man was over 6 feet tall and lived a hunter gatherer way of life, drawing from the resources at hand. It is only the limited diet of the agricultural-based societies that gave us shorter physiques. The change of diet in developing industrial cultures determines the hunter gatherer's stature, but the architecture still suffers the unyielding and fixed strictures of the settler, turning tradition into stone

The Industrial Revolution created a new role for architecture, which was perceived as being terrible and destructive. In the wake of the rapid and all-consuming power of production, the tenets of the Renaissance exploded; religion limping along behind. The factory/office became a temple to the God of Mammon and large chunks of the population were housed in vast cities laid out as scientific justifications for the above. These are all reasons that we now live in a post-industrial age in which architecture lacks the vigour to express a communal poetic relationship with the landscape and allow the individual to journey through it. Architecture can only now reflect the individual's soul and its reading of the world as subject matter. If that soul has no reading then so much the better, for then we can build banal mass-produced reproductions of copies that merely serve to decorate the function of comfort, but with no joy.

Guilt for the change wrought by society upon itself still has little effect in aesthetic policy beyond a concern for the remnants of the American tribes and the Aborigines' humiliation. Travellers and road protesters may still attempt to readdress the balance by reminding us of the importance of landscape and the differences between the routes people may choose to pass along, but essentially the concept of uncontrolled movement is anathema to subtopian society.

Another by-product of industrial mass production and release of labour from the drudgery of making life a matter of survival is the opportunity to make mistakes from experiments: the ability to combine an ever changing array of ingredients to realise any ambition that imagination can make understandable. The Trade Fair and Exposition are examples of occasions when the joy and excitement of structure and programme can be explored. The Crystal Palace and the Festival of Britain, respectively positioned at the blossoming and at the decline of this country's industrial history, sought to express the vigour of technology with a cultural re-examination, to produce situations in which architecture could return to its roots as a reflective mirror of society's beliefs. It is important that the savagery of imagination, too, is not tamed.

The experiments carried out by the students of Unit 3 attempt to bear this out in their application of an imagined future situation (camping in February in English open countryside), with a flexible range of skills and materials available. The imagination of expressing a structural concept is where the individual flavour of the structures shown begins to make the architecture. The possible combinations of the structures, with an urban arrangement in mind, give an uncertain aspect to the eventual placement. The imagination has to be as flexible as the structure is portable, and there is the crux of the dilemma. The intelligence to survive on the move is not judged by physical death, as in the past, but by the public reception of the image it beholds. In reality, the product is of a crude hand-crafted, thrown-together nature on close inspection; but it is one that, regardless, realises the full plethora of architectural potential.

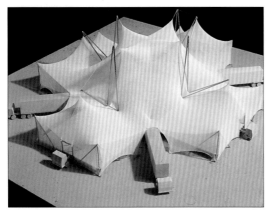

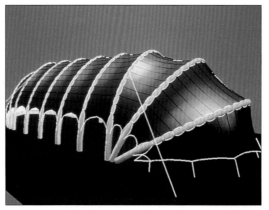

Time for Peace Pavilion, millennium project | *Air-tube supported facility for military operations*

acoustic requirements and the need to provide rain cover for the performers. The design became a mixture of architecture, industrial design, and engineering.

Based on our experience with the Moseley Pavilion, we were asked to design a deployable theatre to serve as a training facility for Cadillac dealers throughout the United States. The enclosed theatre used a blackout membrane which allowed for presentations to an audience of 300 car dealers. Once again, we used a similar tripod system that could be secured on the ground and then lifted up in to position. However, as a value engineering by-product, we opted for the rental of a crane at each site, in lieu of using a self-lifting hydraulic mechanism mounted on the truss masts. Since the facility was to be used for five days in each location, we were able work with a 12-hour total deployment schedule instead of the four-hour schedule for the Moseley Pavilion.

When the Cadillac facility completed its tour, the structural shell of this facility was transformed into the Consumer Pavilion for AT&T Global Olympic Village at Centennial Park for the Atlanta Olympic Games. The theatre became a gallery of high-tech communication systems, including video projection and interactive modules.

The Time for Peace Pavilion is a project for a deployable museum and studio for promoting the concept of peace throughout the world. The original concept is the brainchild of the French artists Robert and Marion Einbeck. Again, using the notion of truck-mounted deployable systems, we developed a facility that uses eight trailer trucks which interconnect and house a series of exhibits, including interactive terminals which demonstrate ideas of peace. With partial sponsorship by the German and Israeli governments and the UN, this project is scheduled to open by the millennium.

The fastest deployable facilities we have created to date are used for military operations. The LANMAS and TME facilities are both air-tube supported structures which use a patterned tensile fabric membrane as lateral support to create a truly synergetic structure with both elements dependent on each other. LANMAS uses a low pressure air system and TME uses a medium pressure system (30 psi) contained within exotic compound fabrics. Both can be erected in less than one hour after initial layout and staking. These systems are to be used for shelters for helicopters and officers' quarters in Desert Storm type applications. What is

different from historical air-tube structures is that the air compressors need not operate constantly once the arches are inflated. The value of deployable structures is beginning to be recognised outside the realms of the theatre and military, and we have begun to work on projects where such facilities have not previously been used; for example, education.

The 'ur-form' of demountable buildings is the circus tent. Some may argue that this is really a deployable building, with elephants and all! However, the circus tent is truly an extraordinary kit of parts that merges building integration in its completed form with an installation process that allows for on-site parallel work. We have been inspired by both the classic European *chapiteau* and the American 'big top', which are designs that have been honed over the past hundred years. Using an evolution of this technology, where the hemp ropes that are sewn into the fabric become web belts with d-rings, the edge ropes become trucking web straps, and the fabric becomes a double-curved stressed skin, rather than cladding on a rope structure. We developed a generation of new rental tents for manufacturers. Starting with the Anchor Module in 1978, the Genesis in 1985, the Century in 1987 and the Tension tent in 1990, we designed these tent systems in the USA and perceive them as the next step in a long tradition.

Using some of these products as the core of demountable facilities has proved fruitful. Twice a year in the centre of New York City, the 7th on 6th Tents for the fashion industry are erected. At this time, Bryant Park in the centre of Midtown Manhattan becomes a one-week-long fashion village with a media centre, dressing rooms, a runway (catwalk) and seating for an audience of 1,200 seats and 600 seats. The tents are standard rental tent products which we had previously designed and the staging is all fabricated from scaffold systems with plywood and a few custom fabric elements for lighting and interior effect. The set-up takes approximately a week and the strike time is about three days.

We have developed the idea of using rental tent technology for custom applications, such as our design for the Ringling Brothers and Barnum & Bailey Travelling Circus, which has a 240 x 356-foot span, and a smaller 120-foot-wide patented design for Clyde Beatly Circus. These designs use a bale ring technology and truss masts to create a usable theatre space after a three-day installation.

JOEP VAN LIESHOUT
In Conversation with Klaar van de Lippe

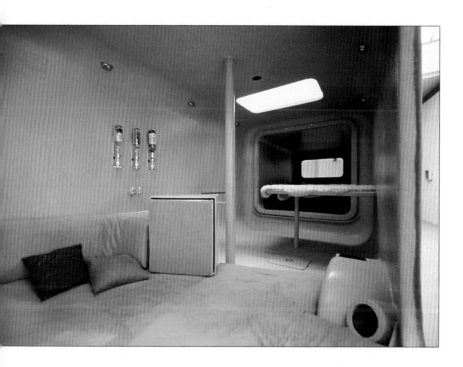

Rotterdam-based Atelier van Lieshout was established in 1995 by the artist Joep van Lieshout (born in Ravenstein, 1963), after he gained, in collaboration with the acclaimed architect Rem Koolhaas, international recognition for the design of several bars and sanitary units for the prestigious Grand Palais in Lille (1994). The artist is currently working on another project with Koolhaas to convert a former bank on 43rd street in downtown Manhattan into a theatre.

Perhaps Van Lieshout's most charismatic work is the creation of a series of provocative mobile homes – *La Bais-o-Drôme*, *Survival Unit Autocrat,* and *Modular House Mobile* – which have inhabited art galleries and roadsides in Cologne, Rotterdam, Reykjavik, Paris, New York, Los Angeles and Winnipeg. Although these trailers do contain pragmatic conveniences, such as toilets, sinks and kitchens, the interiors and exteriors also communicate exotic and romantic ideas about the possibilities for a portable dream home with fur-lined or slick and shiny spaces. The mobile homes are just a part of Van Lieshout's output, which ranges from furniture design to sculpture and environmental installations.

Klaar van de Lippe is an artist and collaborator in Atelier van Lieshout.

Klaar van de Lippe: In your earlier work with crates, and later the furniture, you operated a strict system of measurement. The work was founded on a rigid concept, although very physical in terms of the colours you used and the polyester material. The conceptual aspect now seems to be more a thing of the past. What you're currently making is more organic, more sensitive?

Joep van Lieshout: Yes.

KL: Was this conceptual aspect of your furniture perhaps more based on the production side than on aesthetic conviction?

JL: Hmm.

KL: You first worked under your own name, but some time ago changed it to Atelier van Lieshout. Is the creativity now collective?

JL: Sometimes.

KL: How does it work? Is it an *atelier* in the same sense as the old-fashioned artist's atelier?

JL: Yes.

KL: Thank you. Ah! So the house rules, turn up on time etc, they're the general rules, and then there are the job allocations. Everyone has their own assignment . . . I've got it. And you're the boss?

JL: Yes.

KL: Your own work, or the team's work, is bought by all and sundry and has a practical use as well as being exhibited as art. Do you rate one higher than the other?

JL: Hmm, hmm.

KL: So, is it more a question of people enjoying it?

JL: Yes.

KL: But to keep the business rolling, you must need to earn a lot of money. OK, so in principle you don't make a distinction between art and artifact – does that extend your potential market considerably . . . ?

JL: Yes.

KL: So this lack of distinction has a purely practical side?

JL: Yes.

KL: The things you make are getting bigger and bigger. First it was furniture, then baths and bathrooms, followed by diminutive houses and mobile homes. It will probably be proper houses and buildings next. If someone asked you to construct a building, a prison for instance, would the answer probably be . . . ?

JL: Yes.

KL: There used to be two clear sides: the strict side and the pricks. Let's say the rational and the irrational. I now see more of a mixture. The phalluses are still there, but even the strict things have become more organic. Take the skullrooms, for instance: intuition, desires, and even passions now seem more prominent – are these more important than severe concepts and intellectual reasoning?

JL: Yes.

KL: Yet your/the team's way of working is not woolly. The production methods are, in fact, extremely efficient. There is actually a dichotomy there – I would almost say a romantic capitalist or a practical utopian . . . are you laughing because you're pleased?

JL: Ha, ha, ha!

KL: There is an increasing drive towards autarky: to be self-sufficient, independent. That could be something purely pragmatic, but it could also be an idea that can be taken further; like, for instance, some of those religious sects – the Shakers, for example, whose ideology set them apart. Are you driven by any sort of political or religious conviction?

JL: No.

KL: So the fact that you make your own medicines, bottle your own vegetables, make your own machines – that's all driven by one idea: independence?

JL: Yes.

KL: There is no underlying, larger world-view? There is nothing that you absolutely accept or reject? In fact, you have no morals?

JL: Yes.

KL: That explains a lot of things, because I'm now eating a home-made sausage, from your own slaughtered free-range pigs, as well as some superb bottled vegetables. Very healthy. But you are also plying me with lots of your home-distilled pear brandy.

JL: Delicious isn't it?

KL: These drawings I'm looking at, of factories and machines and all sorts of people at work; sort of settlements, communes . . . only women seem to be working there. Oh no! I can spot a man over there. Are these drawings part of some kind of masterplan? A vision of the future?

JL: [?]

KL: I can't quite figure out whether you are planning one day to live in the kind of community shown in the drawings. I see it more as a romantic ideal than a concrete plan, although you also make guns: that really is for real. Hmm . . . it looks as though you would like to set up your own state; almost as though you're wanting to transform the proverbial artist's individuality from a *state of mind* into a literal *state of being*. Am I right in feeling that?

JL: Yes.

KL: I am suddenly reminded of your early work, when you were still at the academy. You copied Machiavelli's *The Prince* and took photos of yourself as a sad ruler. Has that drive to have your own domain always been there?

JL: [...]

KL: What about those huge beds you're making, and all that polygamy: is that serious? Is it also part of your masterplan?

JL: Yes.

KL: The sexual element is right at the centre; almost as a mainspring, a sort of creative power ... ?

JL: Yes.

KL: But what dimension does that inhabit? Does love also play a part? Is there also a Guinevere, a woman you love and for whom you fight?

JL: [...]

KL: Or does it all revolve round lust? Lust with a capital L?

JL: [...]

KL: Can I take some elixir with me later?

JL: Yes.

KL: Give me the one for uneasiness and vague premonitions, the *sedative tincture*.

March 1998, Rotterdam.

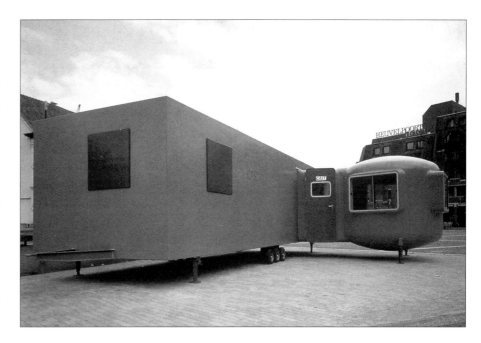

FROM ABOVE: Castmobile, Tilburg, 1996; Information Stand, Aalborg, 1996; Reception Unit, Zürich, 1996

Schräge Ebene *(Sloping Surface), Supersommer, Vienna, 1976*

Rahmenbau *(Frame Building), Documenta 6, Kassel, 1977*

The space of projection

The treatment of the facade as a separate element and as a carrier of content reveals similarities with Venturi's thought that the two-dimensional sign becomes architecture. Like Venturi, HRC accept the facade as the boundary of urban public space, but since Ortner declared monotony to be a design principle, HRC's facades do not transport messages in the Venturian sense but act in the way that independent sculptural elements react to the functional necessities of the building and respect the structural circumstances of the public space.

According to HRC, a visual calming down of the built environment will provide the background and the spaces for urban life and projection. The idea of the matrix and the monument (though not expressed by them explicitly in the early 190s) seemed to develop into an underlying theme of the office buildings that they were designing at that time. In an essay of 1989,[13] Ortner, in relation to the BENE Administration Building, points out that the concrete grid of the facade was meant to represent the building's unfinished character, as well as representing the thinking of its users in laboratory structures.[14]

In HRC's project for a mixed-use building, completed in Berlin in 1989, elements of the temporary architecture and landscape images recur. The building can be categorised into three parts: the red facade as the image, the white building as the carrier of the image, and the structure as the support and sign of 'unfinishedness'. It is important that the facade is not representing anything but itself. In these respects, a direct link to *Schräge Ebene* can be established.

The skin has conceptually detached itself from the architectural construction. It is an independent and flexible medium in the landscape. Via the architectural surface we try to put parts of the old and the new social environment into a new and wholesome context and relation.[15]

The idea of the ephemeral is thus still important in the current work of the individual practices of Günter Zamp Kelp and Ortner & Ortner, being employed as a vehicle to communicate the notion of change and flexibility in society and architecture.

Notes

1 Haus-Rucker-Co, 'Mind Expanding Program', in Dieter Bogner, 'Denkräume-Stadträume 1967-1997', *Haus-Rucker-Co*, Ritter Verlag (Klagenfurt), 1992; trans T Schmiedeknecht.

2 Ibid, p29

3 Ibid.

4 Stanislaus von Moos, 'Kunst und Technik: Direktkoppelungen', Heinrich Klotz, *Haus-Rucker-Co 1967-1983*, Vieweg & Sohn (Braunschweig/Wiesbaden),1984, p7; trans T Schmiedeknecht.

5 HRC in Dieter Bogner, 'Denkräume-Stadträume 1967-1997', op cit, p49.

6 Ibid, p35.

7 Laurids Ortner, 'Zu neuem Raum', in Heinrich Klotz, *Haus-Rucker-Co 1967-1983*, op cit, p90.

8 Manfred Ortner, Margarethe Jochimsen, 'Gespraech am weissen Tisch:

Katalog', *Haus-Rucker-Co, Zeichnungen 1967-74*, Bonner Kunstverein (Bonn), 1975 , p12; trans T Schmiedeknecht.

9 Laurids Ortner,'Konstruktion der zweiten Natur', in Heinrich Klotz, *Haus-Rucker-Co 1967-1983*, op cit, p122.

10 Laurids Ortner, 'Amnestie für die gebaute Realität', *Werk Archithese* 17/18, 1978, p32; trans T Schmiedeknecht.

11 HRC in Dieter Bogner, 'Denkräume-Stadträume 1967-1997', op cit, p97.

12 Ibid, p109.

13 Laurids Ortner, 'Leben im Büro', *Bauwelt 13*, 1989.

14 BENE Administration Building, Waidhaofen, Austria, 1989. Architects: Ortner Architekten, Linz (now Ortner & Ortner Baukunst, Vienna and Linz).

15 Zamp Kelp, *Die Haut als Botschaft, Formalhaut*, Verlag der Georg Büchner Buchhandlung (Darmstadt), 1988, p53; trans T Schmiedeknecht.

GÜNTER ZAMP KELP
In Conversation with Torsten Schmiedeknecht

Torsten Schmiedeknecht: In 'Denkräume-Stadträume' (Thinkspaces-Cityspaces), Dieter Bogner describes the work of Haus-Rucker-Co as consisting of two main areas of interest – *Bewusstseinserweiterung* and *Stadtgestaltung* (expansion of consciousness and shaping of the city):

> Where the first concern shaped the early years in the form of the Mind Expanding Program, the second concern became more evident and gained importance in the theory and practice of the *Provisorische Architektur* (temporary, provisional architecture) from the mid seventies onwards.[1]

According to Bogner, this interest in the expansion of consciousness led to a possible categorisation of areas of interest into utopian, psychological, public and ecological space; whereas 'shaping the city' would mean considering 'city space', 'in-between space' and 'thinking space'. Taking Bogner's analysis into account, I would like to ask you what importance the term ephemeral had for HRC's work, and respectively, its methods of work?

Günter Zamp Kelp: The term ephemeral was of especial importance to us in the early years. *Provisorische Architektur* came about after we had been exploring the ephemeral through our work for several years.

TS: What would you describe as your present definition of the term ephemeral and does it currently have any place or importance in your work?

GZK: In my work, there is a tendency to move from the ephemeral to the static. Nevertheless, in my present work I am always trying to convey elements and experiences from our time as HRC. The use of ephemeral elements, even when it comes to the construction of buildings, still interests me, but a more pragmatic working approach has naturally brought about some restrictions and influenced my practice. Conceptually, nothing much has changed, but of course one cannot approach the realisation of a building in the same free and independent way as in the early HRC days. It was very important for us to test things: you thought of something, designed it, built it and confronted society and the urban dweller with it. If the built project was accepted by the public it remained in its location like the *Rahmenbau* in Kassel, whereas other projects like the *Nike von Linz* were acknowledged with less acceptance, even though some members of the public protested against its dismantling after only two years of its existence on the roof of the art school. Generally, one could say that most of the HRC projects had probably been almost too uncompromising, which inevitably set them within the realm of the ephemeral. At the time, we really weren't interested in how we could sell or exploit our projects commercially. Concepts and realisations were quite uncompromising in most cases. Being convinced ourselves that a project was good was the important thing. Today, I would say that the notion of permanence has to be taken into account.

TS: In the chapter 'Augenblicke städtischer Sinnlichkeit' (moments of urban sensuality), in the 1982 essay 'Journal', you describe three situations that are linked directly with experiencing the urban environment and which could be categorised as ephemeral architecture: the *Mondessen* (Mooneating), instigated in Vienna in 1969 by HRC on the occasion of the landing on the moon; the *Riesenbillard* (Giant Billiard), in Manhattan, 1970; and Magritte's *Le festin de Pierre* of 1943.[2] All three examples show possibilities of experiencing the urban environment sensually.

In *L'horizon negatif* (the negative horizon), Paul Virilio writes about his attempts to manipulate his visual perception by trying to look only at the spaces in-between objects or buildings.[3] In doing so, he tried to avoid the phenomenon of only re-seeing what he had already known and seen before. Virilio states that it enabled him to constantly create new spatial experiences. How do you see the relationship between the expansion of consciousness and sensual urban experiences today, and which appropriate architectural means can be employed in order to expand consciousness?

GZK: The means used within the *Provisorische Architektur* programme (temporary, provisional architecture) or the Mind Expanding Program were to a great extent determined by the time in which these projects were taking place. The expansion of consciousness, in the sense of the 60s, when people were experimenting with the whole realm of perception – be it visual or physical, with or without the use of drugs – is probably no longer necessary.

Today, we are exposed to so many different images and so much information that our awareness and respectively our perception are being expanded almost automatically. If I become aware of my perception, my consciousness or at least my perspective on things also expands. Therefore, I believe that the critical issue today is to find a means of structuring these new phenomena and possibilities of perception. One catchphrase that I like to use in these respects is: 'means of help for a better understanding of the world'. The *Neanderthalmuseum*[4] or the *Jahrtausendblick*,[5] for instance, could be considered as such a means; with their help, aspects of society can be addressed, and where the viewer and the user can be confronted, they can become concerned with these aspects. For me, this means establishing a dialogue between the observation of society, the realisation of projects, and the reaction of society, in dealing with these projects. Operating within the realm between art and architecture is therefore still very important. Thus, the subject matter has remained the same in my work, but the conditions have changed.

TS: HRC's projects within the *Provisorische Architektur* can be seen as 1:1 models set out to test reality. The notion of the process in this work seems very significant. In many of your own texts you emphasise the necessity of constant change in the urban environment. How do you accommodate these notions in a building like the Neanderthal Museum? What role does the site or the place play for you in the conceptual stage of a project?

GZK: What is important to me is the topic, or, if you wish, the theme of a project or task. In this respect, the emphasis of my work has changed. Conveying the metaphor has become a central issue. I try to formulate a building as a whole and to make it express the task. I want the building to have an attitude and to take on a position regarding the brief.

The spiral in the Neanderthal Museum is such a metaphor: its strange appearance accounts for an expression of one possible model representing the development of society. Critically, one could claim that the current model is questionable. The view from the platform at the end of the tangent on top of the spiral is therefore directed into uncertainty. On the other hand, the interior of the museum, which is finished in exposed concrete, refers not only to the natural history of the Neanderthal, which

used to have deep limestone gorges with rivers, but also attempts to create an associative link with the cave out of which man has evolved; the cave as a starting point of our cultural development. Thus the notion of change exists inherently in the project as a metaphor. The communication of the message was a key issue in HRC's work.

Today, I am still trying to confront society with issues through my buildings. Site and place are important to me: the site for the Neanderthal Museum was crucial for the conceptual development of the building, although one never knows whether similar parameters might not be found elsewhere. The translocation with which we are dealing today certainly has to be taken into account. The appearance of the Neanderthal Museum in books, magazines and on television, means that it could almost be transferred to another physical location. The name Neanderthal is instantly associated with a myth linked to the landscape, but the Neanderthal is an ordinary recreational tourist area. The task of the museum is thus to re-establish the lost myth in connection with the specific site. Hence, the alien appearance of the skin, the lack of scale and the lack of openings, in combination with the cave-like character of the interior.

TS: How, in these terms, do you see the constant flood of images to which we are exposed as a problem for the designer, since it surely has become impossible to free oneself from preconceived images?

GZK: The question here concerns the continuing role of architecture. The notion of the site remains important: I would not want to see the same buildings everywhere. I find worrying the current tendency that I can only orientate myself by looking at billboards to discern whether I am in an American or a Chinese metropolis. But a distinction needs to be made between architecture that produces mass and creates an order, and architecture that articulates an idea, thus creating an identity. Not every building can achieve the latter.

TS: The matrix and the monument?

GZK: In a certain sense, yes. But I would still prefer to call it commercial architecture and articulating, topic-related architecture. This also means that size does not matter – you can shake the world with a small building. Large size and mass are definitely important phenomena, though not necessary criteria if something is to have an effect or not. The term 'dynamic' is perhaps more suitable: the smallest building developing some kind of dynamic will always have an effect.

TS: In your text 'Die Haut als Botschaft' (the skin as message) you state that conceptually the skin has detached itself from the architectural construction.[6] Referring to Buckminster Fuller you assert that the minimal description of life is consciousness. Consciousness you split into a system that is becoming conscious and another system that is being perceived. Therefore, in your opinion, consciousness consists of four elements: the observer, the observed, the interrelation between the two, and the nothingness in front of which something is being observed. You argue that the urban landscape becomes legible through its surfaces. How would you distinguish your position from Robert Venturi, who in *Learning from Las Vegas* also states that the two-dimensional sign becomes architecture?[7]

GZK: In HRC's project *Ballon Für Zwei*, the skin and the construction become one with the plastic membrane. In the installation *Schräge Ebene* the surface has been liberated. I am more concerned with the skin or surface than with the two-dimensional sign, even though my understanding of this quite complex area might have changed a little. Skin and surface are important with regard to their role as background for projections. There is a difference though between ephemeral and permanent projections. For example, the painting on the wall behind you is also a permanent projection.

TS: In an essay about your project for the Centre for Art and Media Technology in Karlsruhe you refer to Malevich's *Black Square* and compare it with the television set.[8]

GZK: The *Black Square* contains every possible projection and you can project anything on to it. When one layers an endless number of projections the result is the black square – in the same way as is achieved with paint. The television projects its images on to me, whereas I can use the *Black Square* as a surface for the projection of my own thoughts and ideas. I consider a drawing to be as much a projection (evolving out of myself) as a conventional slide projection – metaphorically, as much as physically. For example, in 1992 I designed a mixed-use house that was supposed to be built in a river landscape near Düsseldorf. I had planned to transfer the features of this landscape on to the building's facade via screen printing, which for me would have also been a projection. Most evident here, is that the surface of the city is the scaffolding for projections.

TS: Are Malevich and the Neanderthal Museum possible projection screens for multiple readings?

GZK: The surface of the Neanderthal Museum is relatively deep (18 centimetres). It consists of two layers of glass: the outer one more translucent, and the inner layer sandblasted. Behind these two layers is situated an aluminium foil that reflects the light hitting the facade. It is difficult to focus on the facade, which emphasises the strangeness and difficulty of categorising what you see. Personally, I consider the facade of the Neanderthal Museum a step forward, especially in terms of its materiality. Through its abstract materiality, its depth and the renunciation to use a recognisable or known image, the facade of the museum allows multiple readings and creates a great number of different moods.

TS: Abstraction as a means to counteract the virtual world of images?

GZK: Abstraction is an important means, maybe the only possible chance to facilitate awareness and to enable us to project different aspects of ourselves.

TS: In his essay 'The Overexposed City' Paul Virilio discusses a shifting of boundaries through telecommunications.[9] The computer screen as interface between man and machine replaces the role of the facades of buildings as surfaces of property allotment.

> Telecommunications promote the merger of disconnected metropolitan fringes into a single urban mass . . . Each surface is an interface between two environments that is ruled by a constant activity in the form of an exchange between the two substances placed in contact with one another.[10]

For Virilio, therefore, the decisive surface today is the screen. He claims that the opacity of building materials has been reduced to zero, which is best expressed by looking at the change of city boundaries, shifting from having been the palisades to being the screen today. Neil Leach in critically approaching Virilio asks:

> Has the homogenisation of global communications the counter effect of a renewed celebration of the specificity of material place?[11]

How would you define your own position?

GZK: In principle, I would agree with Neil Leach, but I don't think we are dealing with the traditional notion of space here. This traditional notion has to be challenged and developed further: for instance, through buildings like museums that are capable of highlighting certain ideas and of producing an identity – thus establishing links between the physical and the virtual world.

TS: The Matterhorn project of 1974 illustrates HRC's concern with the problem of authenticity. You came to the conclusion that this mountain no longer existed; that the real Matterhorn exists in the form of millions of postcards and photographs. You described a phenomenon that now dominates our visual experiences daily. According to Jean Baudrillard we live in a simulacrum and it has become impossible to trace the origins of anything.

GZK: The power of the images that we consume daily is enormous. But I might almost say that the more enormous this power is, the greater the chances of counteraction. Of course, architecture has to deal with these phenomena but I don't think that physical architecture will eliminate itself. Rather, I think that within the polarity of the virtual and physical worlds there are great possibilities for architecture.

TS: Would you agree that with projects such as *Architekturschleuder*, *Mind Expander* or *Environment Transformer* you created, in a sense, forerunners of virtual reality?

GZK: In a way, yes. Such a forerunner was the *Ballon für Zwei*: the first object that was presented under the name of Haus-Rucker-Co to the public in October 1967, Vienna. It appeared six times between 12.00 am and 6.00 pm on a Wednesday or Thursday through a window of a Viennese *Gründerzeit* facade.[12] Each appearance lasted for about 10 minutes, creating the opportunity for a male/female couple to experience the surrounding urban environment through the tattooed, transparent membrane of the spherical balloon. In *Ballon für Zwei* and *Environment Transformer* the membrane was situated between the organ of visual perception (the eye) and the environment. This obstruction or hindrance was aimed at the relearning of perception.

The impression and the notion of floating dematerialisation and virtuality is also conveyed by the *Gelbes Herz* (Yellow Heart), a pulsating space for two people, which was supposed to change its dimensions. So the intended reactivation of perception was accompanied by transformed impressions of the surrounding environment, which one could experience as being virtual.

TS: In a former text you describe how the use of the Environment Transformers in New York created a link with Vienna, because you had experienced the same strange effects there by perceiving the world through the same apparatus.

GZK: Naturally, you always carry a kind of personal world around with you that attempts to establish links. However, in the case that you just described it was sort of a reverse effect.

TS: Bernard Tschumi formulated the notion of the event in architecture: the event as the place of the combination of difference; architecture not about the conditions of design but about the design of conditions. In 'Monument oder Ereignis' you state that space has lost its claim for finality.[13] Buildings no longer remain monuments but become events. Change and identity replace static order systems. How important are programme and layering for you as a means of spatial manipulation without design?

GZK: Are they not always present anyway? Through my presence, whatever I do, I will always manipulate space. The same accounts, of course, for the event.

TS: But how do you see the attitude of contemporary architects who propose simple shells and leave the programme to sort out the rest?

GZK: I would not necessarily say that this is the wrong attitude, even though it provides an easy route for mediocrity. Some architects today simply argue that there is too much going on anyway. They try to react with simplicity and I do partly find that legitimate. But it is indeed always a question of the brief, and the differences in briefs are enormous. I believe that there must be a space for strong and individually expressive buildings which, if they are strong enough, can relate to the public. If content and building create a strong context there will always be public acceptance. The Neanderthal Museum had 250,000 visitors in one year. Such mechanisms should be used to create and sell a certain quality of architecture. It means that without having to build fairground architecture a broad acceptance within society can be achieved, and buildings – for example museums – act like regulators in the urban fabric. In this sense, I am absolutely for a programme-specific architecture. Regarding the mass of virtual impressions – anything without a certain profile will not last.

TS: Which systems of order do you regard as useful and applicable when you are dealing with the city?

GZK: Cities will, more than is already the case, try to make their name. This is where I see great opportunities for architecture. One phenomenon of architecture is surely that it covers such a huge field of different issues and also levels of quality and that it has to do a lot with politics. The question for me is whether society and politics will start to deal with decent quality to a larger extent. The most simple form here might be the choice of a specific architecture commissioned from a specific architect. On a larger, more strategic scale, I can imagine a City of Scientists or a City of Artists. Instead of the rather superficial label that Düsseldorf employs for itself as the city of artists, for example, the profile would have to be the programme and vice versa.

This is where architecture could come into account again. I still believe that it has a shaping impact on society: look at Berlin and Vienna. In Berlin there is a lot of dereliction as a result of the war. The structure is entirely different to that of Vienna, where you can still almost literally touch the monarchy with both hands. This indicates that there are specific hierarchies in place, a phenomenon that does not exist any more in Berlin. Vienna has quite a lot of substance, and accordingly much tradition. In Berlin, they are now trying to re-establish tradition by means of reconstruction – the wrong method, in my opinion. I think architecture should aspire to be a bit more up-to-date; the development at Potsdamer Platz is very ordinary. The architects could have become more involved: the design and layout of the public zones on ground-floor level lack any kind of complexity.

TS: So you think it is just the production of mass?

GZK: In some ways, yes. But it is not necessarily the fault of the architect who designed Potsdamer Platz; perhaps more a problem of urban planning and realisation in general, and the fact that the process of production of architecture has to be assessed again. The structure and build-up of this process has to become much more complex, such as in the film industry where team work and responsibility comes naturally. In architecture, the architect is always the front man and carries far too many responsibilities. These responsibilities should be shared with all the other experts. Our professional culture is a monoculture and this is wrong. The profession is outmoded, which might relate to the problem that everybody within it thinks that they can produce great architecture. Yet this conviction is untenable when it comes to complex briefs. Shouldn't one of the objectives be the ability to consciously express an idea in a complex building? In these respects, I think that Potsdamer Platz is a missed opportunity, as a result of the fear in the world of politics of processes that might be too complex.

TS: Finally, how do you see the future of the city?

GZK: The future of the city is a fascinating subject. I believe that the physical aspect will always claim its stake. The development of the urban environment takes places in wave-like movements. The media and its impact is highly rated at the moment, but I imagine that its attractiveness might be lost at some point. The development of city and social space will always have to do with perception. The question is how we learn to deal with certain phenomena of perception.

Remember the railways: in the early days, people didn't know how to deal with the landscape that was racing past the compartment window, so they would avert their eyes and read instead. After a while, it appeared normal to them that if you moved between two places what you would see in the middle was the landscape racing by. The same problem applies today. Man will develop an attitude towards these new phenomena of perception that will enable him to deal with them, and to relate them to the physical social space. This will of course have consequences. Perhaps at some point it will cause the end of the total mobility that exists today. This might coincide with changes in the form of simulations and implantations of the local scenery, as a temporary exit from normal society.

Düsseldorf, Germany, 27 February 1998

Notes

1 Dieter Bogner, *Denkräume-Stadträume*, Ritter Verlag (Klagenfurt), 1992.
2 Günter Zamp Kelp, 'Journal', *Haus-Rucker-Co 1967-1983*, Heinrich Klotz (ed), Vieweg (Braunschweig/Wiesbaden), 1984.
3 Paul Virilio, *L'horizon negatif*, Editions Galilée (Paris), 1994.
4 Neanderthal Museum, Mettmann, 1996; architects: Günter Zamp Kelp and Julius Krauss/Arno Brandlhuber.
5 *Jahrtausendblick, steinzeichen steinbergen*, Expo 2000 Hanover; architect: Günter Zamp Kelp.
6 Günter Zamp Kelp, 'Die Haut als Botschaft', *Formalhaut*, Verlag der Georg Büchner Buchhandlung (Darmstadt), 1988.
7 Robert Venturi, *Learning from Las Vegas*, (Cambridge, Mass), 1972.
8 Günter Zamp Kelp, 'Architektur und Medialität', *Daidalos* 35, March 1990.
9 Paul Virilio, 'The Overexposed City', *Lost Dimensions; Semiotext(e)* (New York), 1991; trans Daniel Moshenberg.
10 Ibid.
11 Neil Leach (ed), *Rethinking Architecture*, Routledge (London), 1997.
12 *Gründerzeit*: 1871-73, a period when many industrial firms were found in Germany and Austria.
13 Günter Zamp Kelp, 'Monument oder Ereignis', *Daidalos* 40, June 1991.

TOYO ITO

ITM BUILDING
Matsuyama, Shikoku

The ITM Building is the office of a well-known Japanese confectioner, located in the city of Matsuyama on the island of Shikoku. Architecturally, it represents an important step in Ito's quest for the mastery of material means through rarefaction of space and form. With regard to the latter, this building denotes an interesting parallel to the Shimosuwa Municipal Museum, which preceded it in construction by a year.

Notwithstanding the different context and more prominent location of the museum, and the fact that it embodies a very different programme and purpose, a conceptual analogy can be drawn between the two buildings in relation to the phenomenal dissolution of architectural form. However elusive and tenuous the form of the museum, it appears nevertheless to be sustained by the underlying consciousness of its physical inevitability.

In comparison, the ITM Building emerges as a translucent liquefied structure with no formal will of its own. The form invokes a sense of being generated not through the construction but by the containment of liquid matter within the urban void of the site; kept in place, as it were, by the osmotic resistance of an invisible perimeter membrane.

This effect is, primarily, conveyed by the subtlety of the facade articulation: in its constricted planar three-dimensionality, matter and topography merge into a homogeneous, yet depth-wise, ever shifting substance. The three- and two-dimensional worlds intersect creating a mesmerising effect: a section (the hypothetical one, as if made through a liquid body) where surface is revealed as a condition of the depth it holds within, rather than its planar extension.

Consequently, the ITM Building never materialises as an object. It unfolds as a negative dimension, a reversed form and substance which in the place of its origin, the subtracted part of the city, does not close the gap and mend the fabric but, instead, builds an aperture into a parallel and heretofore unknown dimension of space latent in the site.

With this project, Ito has succeed in approximating a point of semantic dissolution of the idea of facade, while not dispelling the dialectics of inside and outside. More correctly, it is within the withering of the facade's demarcating function as a corollary of its dissolved state that the actual design motive can be found. It renders problematic the topological certainty of the two dialectical positions, inside and outside; whereby their relation is made more complex and provocative.

Conceptually, such a situation is analogous to a glove turned inside out halfway. Its body-making membrane inscribes a continuous surface which folds over itself, exposing the interior and encapsulating the exterior but never quite completely. In consequence, the two sides become contained, one within the other; erasing the possibility of topological differentiation of inside and outside. They merge into a perplexing sameness of being – simultaneously both.

In such an uprooted semantic context the glove membrane imposes itself as an object of aberrant intensity. This intensity, however, is not born out of the object's capacity to recall the original configuration, but the paradox of its muted physical state, in which neither form nor substance are constant and matter is seduced into existence as its own impending negation.

The ITM facade is an instrument that changes the order of things while remaining alluringly tentative in its own material presence.

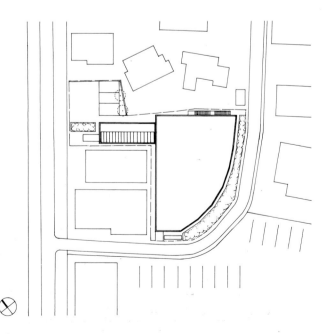 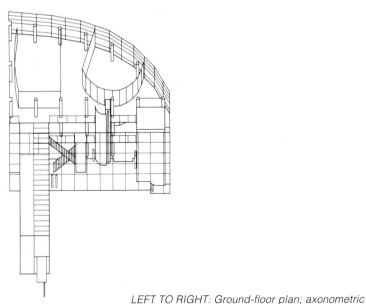

LEFT TO RIGHT: Ground-floor plan; axonometric

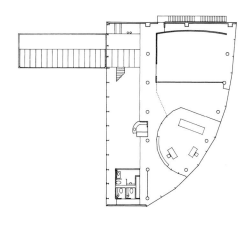

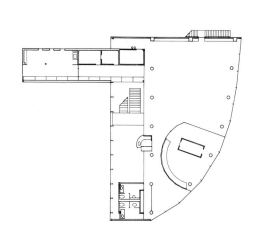

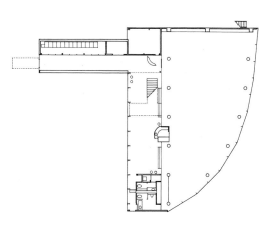

FROM ABOVE: Third-floor plan; second-floor plan; first-floor plan

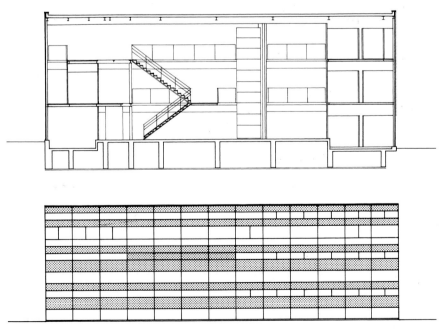

FROM ABOVE: Section; elevation

Seen in such a light, in spite of its disarming formal simplicity, the ITM building unfolds into a labyrinthine structure. This is even conveyed by the way in which the building is entered. Its entrance is located at the back, away from the street; to be happened upon by chance – encapsulated in a discrete metal object whose bowels hold the secret of a passage to the undisclosed interior place.

Invisible from the entrance side due to the site configuration, the main building is never experienced as an object prior to being entered. It materialises as a pure interiority, as its own autonomous territory that gathers at the point where the lag of the entry space wears out. At the same time, that which discloses itself as interior (space) is only conditionally so. Its configuration and scale remain corresponsive to the ordering of the outside world and thus inscribe a parallel counter-place – a reverse urban topos – of the city. This is kept in its place by the depth of the translucency of glass and the density of the delayed time entrapped in the long walls of the entry space.

The interior space draws its conceptual configuration from ideas introduced in Ito's 'T' Building project, completed in Tokyo in 1989. In general, the two projects share a number of other similarities such as the strategy of volumetric composition, plan organisation, and the building-type idea. However, their critical connection resides in the attempt to rarefy and phenomenally transform the space by making it a function of the radiance of intervening matter, rather than exactness of Cartesian geometry.

In the 'T' Building, the space emerges as an effect of the modulated transmission of light and views through the glass facade wall, controlled by the alteration of its translucent and transparent properties. Although free from physical boundaries, such space still remains ordered by a sense of gravity embedded in the visual referencing of the outside world.

The uniform translucency of the exterior wall of the ITM Building, by comparison, constitutes an instrument of the 'ungrounding' of interior space. By reducing the outside world to a mute shadow and diffusing natural light into a luminous presence, Ito creates a condition in which space descends upon itself as a temporal construct. It unfolds as a spectrum of transitory interference between light and matter where no other is given; gravity and geometry included, exist. Consequently, the ground has become inscribed with the precariousness of a trapeze-like structure, liberating the body into a 'levitational' state of being free from the gravitational resistance of space.

Hence, the labyrinthine condition, not only relates to the topological ordering of space but to the enigma of its very nature. In the ITM Building, Ito's spatial metaphors of 'vortex' and 'current' have reached their most tangible embodiment yet, in his pursuit of the technologically-induced changing realities of space and architectural matter.

Vladimir Krstic

TOYO ITO

SHIMOSUWA MUNICIPAL MUSEUM
Nagano

The question of programme continues to be an open issue in Ito's work; open in a sense of the uncertainty of its driving presence in design generation. This is not to say that the programme is necessarily disregarded, rather that it is transcended: that architecture is centred in the pursuit of an idea, of an architectural occasion that arises out of its own place and its own circumstances, whereby the programme is not understood as a given condition but as one that is arrived at.

To that extent, the possibility of an *architecture parlante* (if this ever existed in Ito's work) is short-circuited by the contemplation of the site as a fiction: as a seat of the fictional narratives latent in the very air that surrounds it, whose elusive incarnation in matter and space is made into the primary subject of architectural creation.

Shimosuwa Municipal Museum is inscribed as such through the programmatic default – the antithetical reversal and the dissolution of the didactic narrative associated with the idea of a cultural institution. In respect of this, the factual presence of a cultural artifact is juxtaposed to, or contested by, the ethereal experience of the place itself: what makes it a municipal museum is not what it holds within, but what it enables to be felt, imagined and experienced in the topological sense as an extension of its locus.

For Ito, the understanding of the function of a museum seems to have been grounded in the idea of the repository of memory: memory not born out of, or confined to, mnemonic objects but a poetic state of mind where remembrance and imagination overlap and are indistinguishable, and where time is measured by movement rather than depth.

The convex parabolic arch of the building recalls its lakeside situation. The immaculate geometric precision of the structure resonates abstractness, evocative of an overturned boat or a crest of a wave, yet neither. The metaphor is never complete. It never gives itself up – incessantly enticing and eluding the observing eye. At the very moment it is about to take root in the retina, the metal shape of the building dissolves into an amorphous mirage of a silky vapour that glides weightlessly in its place like an endless image residue caught in the ripples of the water surface.

The difference between the lucidity of the building form (its geometric presence and execution) and the tenuousness of its skin material demarcates poignantly the high act of Ito's performance of architectural magic. Although painstakingly devised, the form is precluded from actualising as an absolute given by the very substance that renders it present: the fleeting materiality of the aluminium surface.

Absent of material gravity, the polished surface of the aluminium shell comes into being at a precarious point in which its molecules intersect with the atmospheric light inscribing the reflective void of its own bodily substance. It neither is nor is not materialising as an optical instance of a topological split between reflection and the surface within which it is contained. In response to these conditions, the geometry of the building form no longer holds as a frame that binds a figure. Instead, it is transformed into a threshold from where the form unfolds on its own.

By creating a dialectical gap between the geometry and the phenomenal substance of the building form, Ito has transformed the reality of an architectural whole into fiction, situating its resolution within the boundaries of the retinal rather than the material world. However, what has been transformed in the Shimosuwa Municipal Museum is more than the perceptual reality of an architectural object – it is precisely the concept of the museum that has undergone radical dissection.

It could be argued that the purpose of a museum in conceptual terms is to provide a frame of reference for the authentication of reality – placement within such a frame automatically confers the status of real and authentic upon an

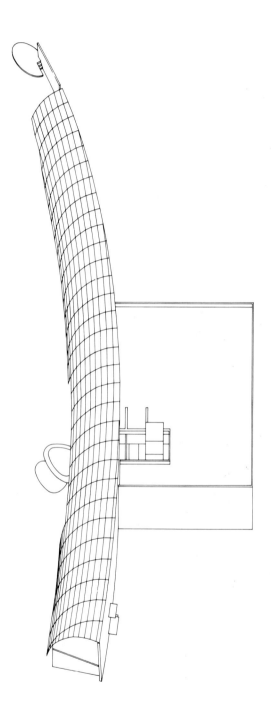

Axonometric

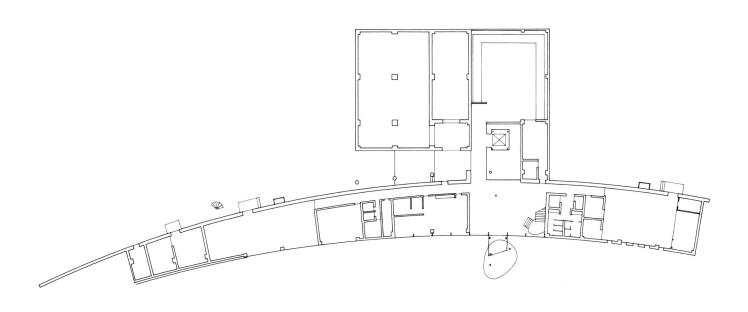

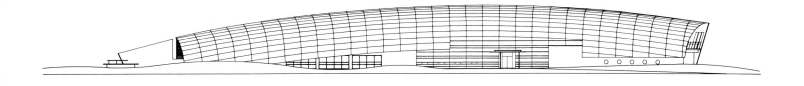

FROM ABOVE: First-floor plan; elevation

artifact. In turn, as a precondition and the consequence of its referencing function, the museum itself comes to be founded in the material veracity of its own existence. To inscribe the museum as a physically elusive structure entails its conceptual reconfiguration into a permeable locus where the capacity to mediate the real becomes debased.

Consequently, the Shimosuwa Municipal Museum transpires as stage rather than a frame of reference that contains and preserves. Its space constitutes a theatre of the eclipse of the real, whose unclaimable ground spells the occurrence of that which cannot be; a place where fiction converges with matter and the measure of truly existing is found in the captured instant of an optical sensation.

The fiction of the water embodies the most obsessive subject of architectural exploration in the Shimosuwa Municipal Museum – not only as an extension of the idea of place, but more so as a matrix for probing into perceptual limits of matter and space in creating architecture. What makes Ito's architecture genuine on its own terms is his uncanny ability to studiously intersect an abstract idea with matter and uncover, within the resonance of the latter, the possibility of an architectural incarnation.

The rarefied ground plane of the museum and its alchemic conversion into an aberration of the endless lake surface is the result of a laborious construction process: searching for the reflective properties of stone and water, the depth of the translucency of glass and opacity of colour, and working out the geometry of relations that enables these elements, through the mediation of light, to produce a different dimension of spatial experience. However, the paradox of this meticulous construction process, and its profound artfulness, is found in the lyrical intent to give material form to the non-existing: an inhabitable fictional space of fluidity that liberates not only the eyes but the body into a daydream of non-gravitational existence.

In the end, neither the object nor its space offer a foothold in the material realm. They float about each other as two fictitious structures: never coming together nor drifting apart; kept in suspense by an undisclosed gravitational force. The completion of the circle remains entrusted to the observing mind, to ponder each time anew and marvel at the museum that harbours the vacuity of the intangible – the memory and the longing of the lake.

Vladimir Krstic

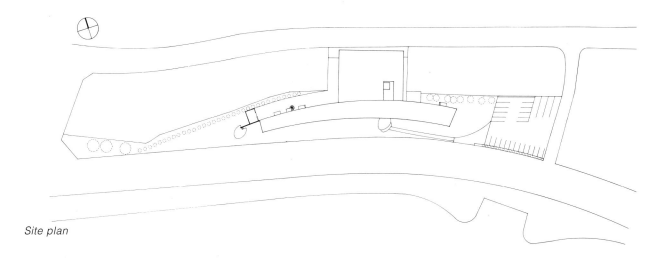

Site plan

GÜNTER ZAMP KELP AND JULIUS KRAUSS/ ARNO BRANDLHUBER

NEANDERTHAL MUSEUM
Mettmann, Germany

When asked which architectural means he considers to be appropriate to counteract the virtual world of images Günter Zamp Kelp states:

> Abstraction for me is an important means, maybe the only possible chance to allow us to become aware of different aspects and to enable us to project ourselves.

The Neanderthal Museum was completed in October 1996, designed in collaboration with Julius Krauss and Arno Brandlhuber. It lies not far from Düsseldorf, Germany, in the Neander Valley, named after the remains of the skeleton that was found there in a cave in 1856. The project is a fine example of the way in which the means of abstraction can be employed in conjunction with a metaphorical interpretation of a brief to create a unique sense of identity and place.

Whether one reads into the building's alien appearance the character of the cave, employs the spiral as a symbol for the development of man, or interprets it as a metaphor for the valley; or perhaps notes its similarity to an amoeba (probably not coincidentally the Greek word for change), it is impossible to categorise the building with a standard description or to place it within a common typology.

The Neanderthal itself is a typical recreational tourist area, and the new building is situated next to the customary bars and hotels that employ the 'vernacular tourist' style of building. These tourist venues seem to proclaim the eternally present 'Gemütlichkeit' that foreign tourists are apparently so keen to find in Germany. (There is even a Neanderthal man on display in a cave in one of the restaurant venues.)

The contrast between the two forms of architecture and display could not be stronger, conflicting with the preconceived images that the tourists bring along, expecting a mixture of ruggedness and Gemütlichkeit. Within the Venturian environment of applied signs that have become architecture but failed to distinguish the Neanderthal from any other natural tourist site, the museum allows the place to recreate its own story through the sophisticated application of form and material.

The story the building communicates is one of change and development. It is the story of infinity and tells of freedom of interpretation, communicated both on a direct level – through the possibility of multiple readings of its material nature – and on a metaphorical level through the architect's choice of materials and method of spatial arrangement.

Günter Zamp Kelp states that there is a third category of space complementing the geometrical and the biological space: 'the space of projection'. The museum with its strange green-glass skin, which reflects and absorbs light simultaneously, operates at the fringe between the realms of physical and projectional space.

In contrast to the competition entry that was originally awarded second prize – in which the spiral had been planned as a narrow passage surrounding three towers (therefore allowing the visitor to choose which route to take) – the spiral, as built, is a broad ramp that accommodates the exhibition. It leads the visitor to the viewing platform that overlooks the valley; offering a view into uncertainty, as described by Günter Zamp Kelp.

The spiral arrangement encourages the visitor to constantly make non-chronological cross-references: by looking across the central staircase to the ascent or descent opposite, an individual pattern of man's history may be constructed while forging new links with the present and future. Such impressions are not unlike ideas expressed in the work of artists such as Dan Graham or Gordon Matta-Clark; explained thus by Walter Benjamin in 1937:

> Historicism presents an eternal image of the past, historical materialism a specific and unique engagement with it . . . The task of historical materialism is to set to work an engagement with history original to every new present. It has recourse to a consciousness of the present that shatters the continuum of history.[1]

According to Zamp Kelp, the Neanderthal Museum acts as a means of providing a better understanding of the world and offers an open interpretation of the past, present and future. This leaves room for curious speculations and discoveries and does not leave the contemporary model of society's development unquestioned. Most interesting in these respects is the fact that there still remains a controversial debate about the taxonomic classification of the Neanderthals, both having been classed as a separate species: Homo neanderthalensis and alternatively as a subspecies of Homo sapiens.

Torsten Schmiedeknecht

Note

1 Walter Benjamin 'Eduard Fuchs, Collector and Historian (1937)', *One-Way Street and Other Writings*, trans Kingsley Shorter, New Left Books (London), 1979, p352.

63

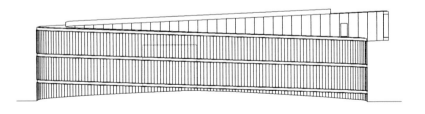

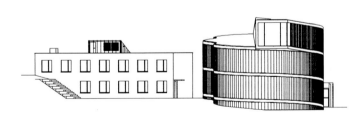

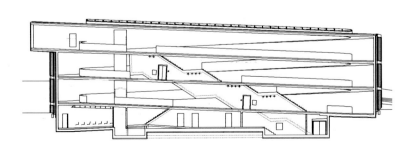

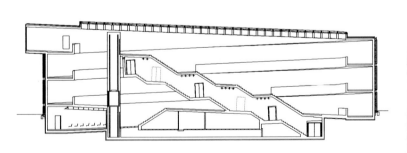

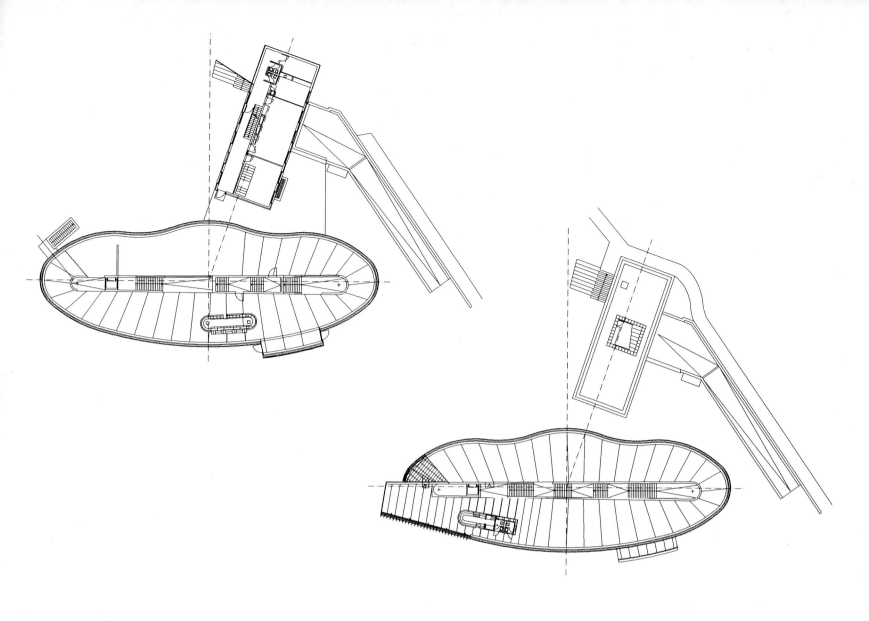

*OPPOSITE: Elevations and sections;
FROM ABOVE: Ground-floor plan;
second-floor plan*

GÜNTER ZAMP KELP
MILLENNIUM VIEW STONESIGNS
Steinbergen, Germany

The craftsman travelling from place to place was communicative. On his way he acquired information and on his journey he passed it on through society. Hiking as the 'miller's pleasure' in the still popular song has also been allocated there to the stones travelling along the beds of rivers, forced by the energy of water. One day, when the stones have left the realm of the waters, they will come to rest in the gravel pit, smooth, rounded and in large numbers.
Günter Zamp Kelp

In the course of history, the rocks of Schaumburg Quarry in Steinbergen have passed through the hands of men who broke the stone from its geological formations to use it all over the world as a building material. The quarry will be fully exploited in about 15 years and although large areas are already overgrown, traces of the workings will serve as reminders of this place as a starting point for an evolution of physical social space.

Designed for EXPO 2000 in Hanover, this project guides the visitor along a pathway that allows the history and nature of stone to be experienced in connection with our cultural history: incorporating various installations such as 'flock of stones', 'solar forests' or 'stone school', in addition to a crater that symbolises the power of architectural intervention.

The pavilions are defined by green glass and stone walls and have a narrative quality that enables different aspects of our cultural development to be suggested; for example, in House of Life, House of Time, House of the Senses.

The climax is the *Jahrtausendblick* (millennium view): a sculptural staircase construction on the ridge of the highest rock wall that acts as a symbol for the whole site. This will be built from the quarry's cyclopian quadrates, terminating in a viewing platform perpendicular to the direction of climbing. The cantilevered platform is set within a steel structure into which are integrated 10 glass frames. Their parallel setting defines views across large areas of landscape to the north and south.
Torsten Schmiedeknecht

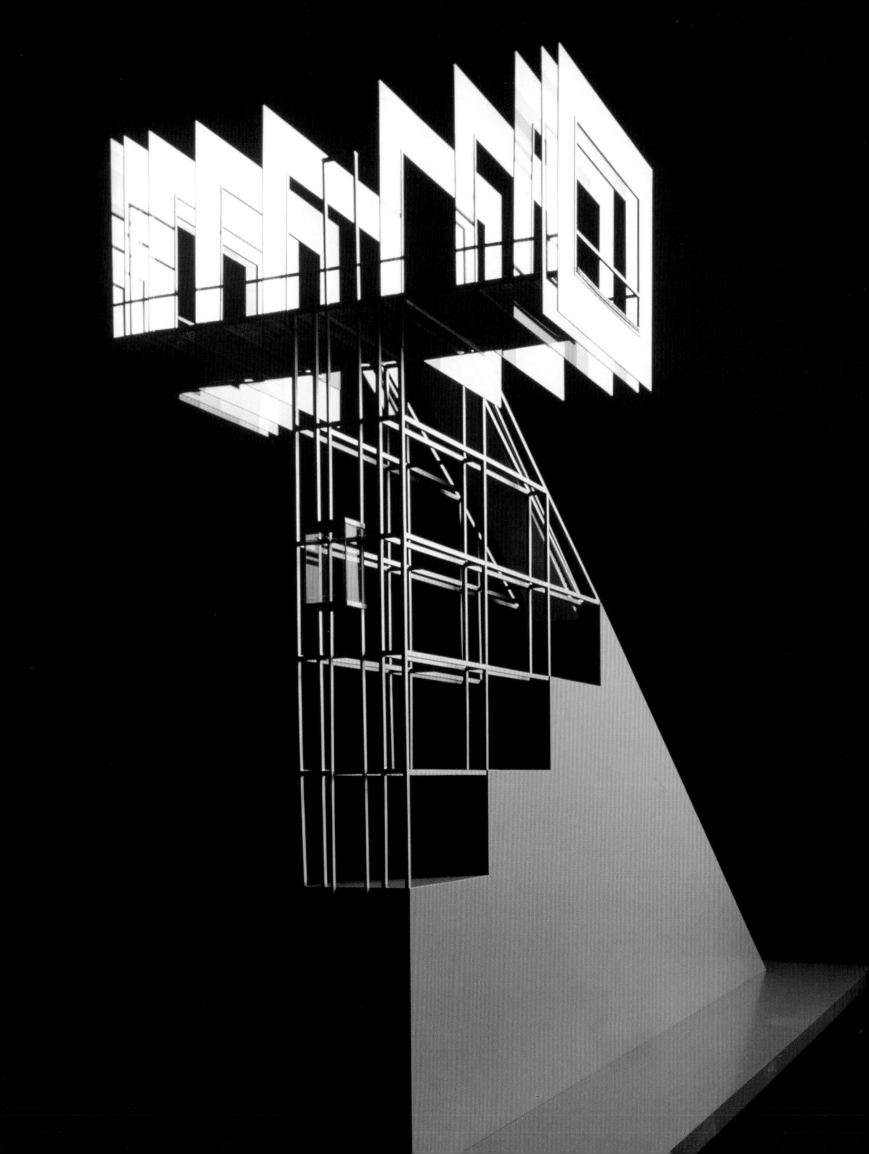

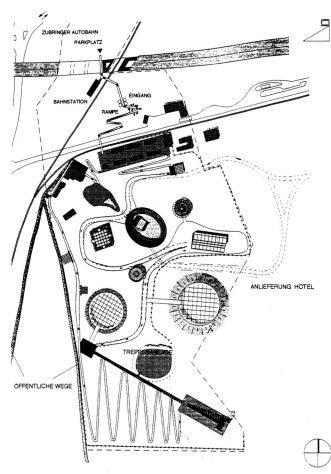

OPPOSITE: Computer rendering of Jahrtausendblick
*(millennium view); FROM ABOVE, L TO R: Model;
photo-montage of site; site plan*

Computer-generated images of solar forest and pavilions

Computer-generated images of observatory and 'Spacehenge'

APICELLA ASSOCIATES
THE COMMUNICATOR

The Communicator is a 3,252-square-metre arena designed to accommodate international corporate communication events in the UK and Europe. The client, WCT Live Communications, requested in its brief an imposing structure that would enhance the social and networking dimension of modern corporate communication methods through a series of flexible internal environments in an entirely mobile structure.

The design is one of the most ambitious of its kind ever proposed, in that it includes sophisticated interior systems. that enable it to be used for a wide range of functions, yet still have the benefits of a minimal deployment time.

The structure employs a central steel mast braced by steel cabling to support an array of extruded aluminium portal frames that carry an insulated PVC roof membrane. This strategy is crucial in order that the entire structure can be erected in a maximum of seven days. The building envelope is completed by an aluminium system floor with associated ramps and access stairs, and interlinked GRP wall panels around the perimeter. The walls could also be used for product and corporate branding and graphic imagery.

The interior components are also part of the architect's proposal and employ a standard motorised wall-panel system (used for reliability and economy), modified to create a reception hall, presentation theatre, seminar rooms and demonstration environments. Each of these may be manipulated to meet the changing demands of diverse audiences, in accordance with regional and international as well as functional variations.

At night, the entire structure is designed to take advantage of the darkness and glows like an ethereal beacon; indeed, the building's form is definitive of a focal point rather than contained: a strategy particularly suited to its purpose but also its condition as a non-site-specific object.
Robert Kronenburg

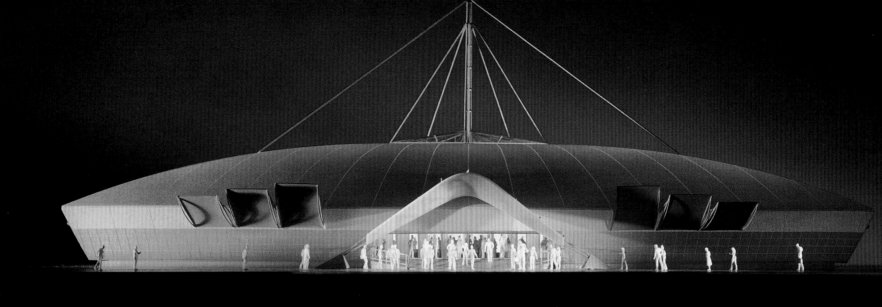

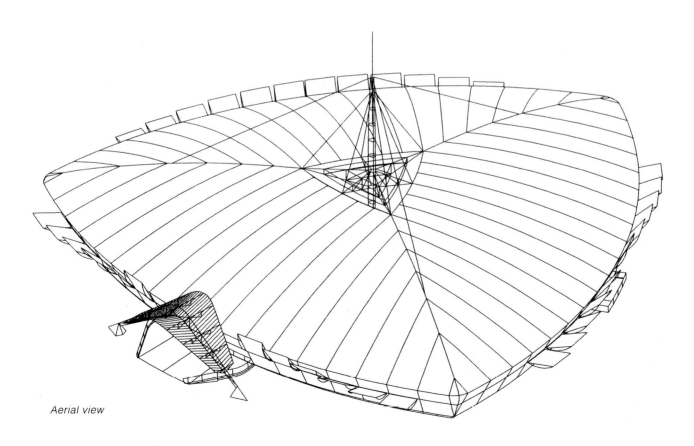

Aerial view

74

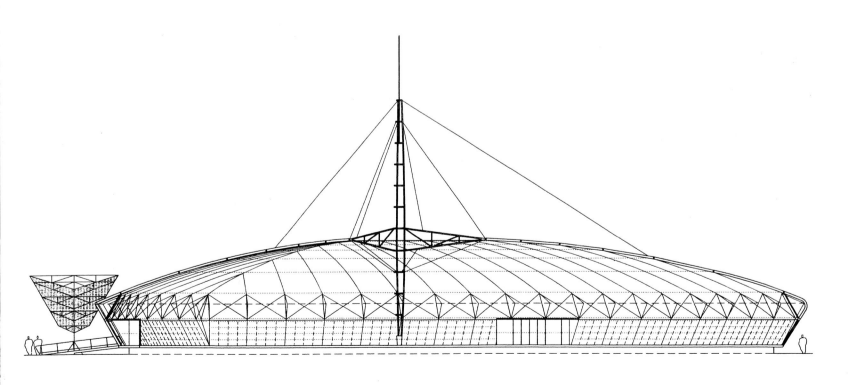

Section

75

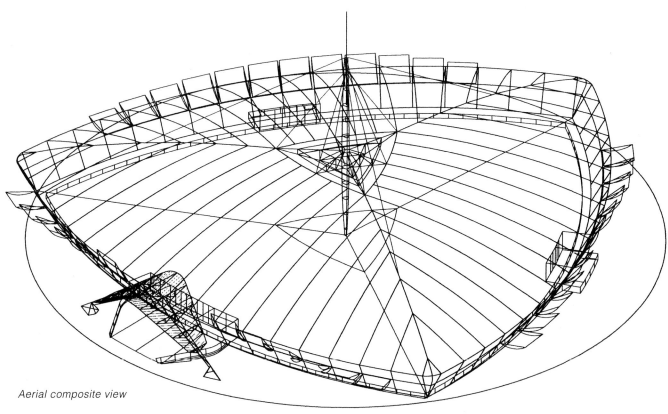

Aerial composite view

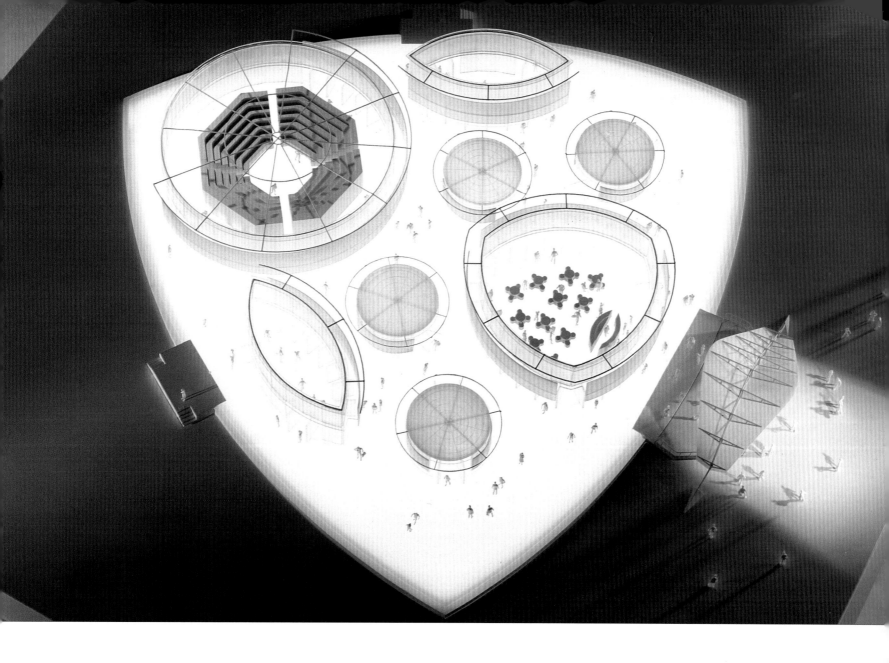

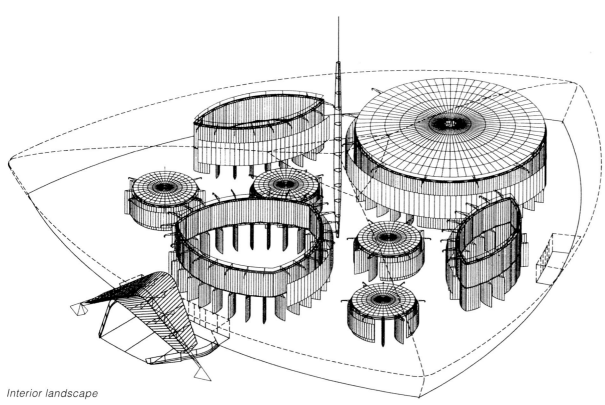

Interior landscape

APICELLA ASSOCIATES AND MARK FISHER
PEPSI BLUE LAUNCH ENVIRONMENT

This architect-designed launch event explores the blurred line between event 'architecture', staging, and the creation of physical man-made objects designed for practical purposes. It was designed as part of a media event in 1996 to bring to public attention the change of Pepsi's branding from its traditional, predominantly red colour to blue. The company believed that this would signify a renaissance for the product and make clear the distinction from Coca-Cola, its greatest rival.

The objective of the brief was to create a one-off event that was based on the theme 'the world turns blue'. This was presented to an audience of 400 people (media, management and distribution) in an aircraft hangar at Gatwick Airport

The event had to be so powerful that it would create immediate newsworthy material to launch a new advertising campaign across Europe, through television, film, print and events sponsorship. Stagecraft, product design, graphics and the manipulation of built form all played a part in the creation of this event.

The audience, who were experienced in the world of promotion techniques, were brought to a fairly remote hangar where they would undoubtedly be expecting a dramatic presentation of some sort. The challenge was to surprise them and to create images and events that would reverberate around the world through the news media and still retain something of the power of the original presentation. The event planning therefore began with the creation of an auditorium space that was simple, plain and enclosed, with raked-seating facing a stage; from where, initially, a corporate presentation on marketing strategy was given.

These preliminaries culminated in the effect of the gauze walls of the space being back-lit to reveal a blue cityscape beyond. The gauze was then flown above the set to reveal a series of apparently static structures that formed the backdrop for the dramatic appearance of three personalities who woould endorse Pepsi Blue: Cindy Crawford rode onto the stage on the back of a Harley Davidson; André Agassi appeared to abseil on to the set from a helicopter above; and Claudia Schiffer appeared in silhouette, apparently from behind a shower curtain, to glide down an elaborate spiral staircase.

To the audience, these photo opportunities seemed to be the climax of the show until the presenter reappeared to explain how short the time would be to take this launch campaign across Europe, stating that there was only one possible way to do it. At this point the whole set began to pull apart: the huge projection screen was pivoted upwards and finally, with a great fanfare, the stages opened right out to reveal Concorde painted in Pepsi Blue livery.

The true star of the proceedings, therefore, turned out to be an object rather than a celebrity. The cameramen and audience rushed ahead to gain new photo opportunities of the three celebrities on the access steps to the aeroplane, and TV and radio interviews were held against the background of Concorde and the remains of the exploded set.

The next day, pictures of the Pepsi Blue Concorde made it into all of the daily newspapers, including broad sheets such as *The Guardian*, in which it was illustrated on the front page in colour. For a single day (therefore ephemeral, in the most accurate sense) this environment was, for those concerned, part of world events.

Robert Kronenburg

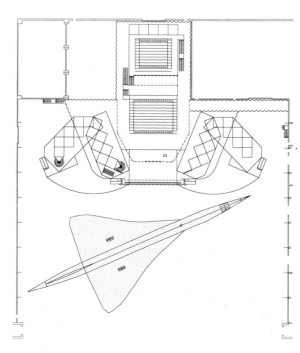

LEFT TO RIGHT: Presentation drawing of Cindy Crawford, André Agassi and Claudia Schiffer emerging from the Concorde; plan

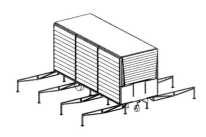
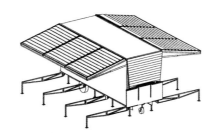
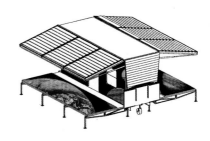
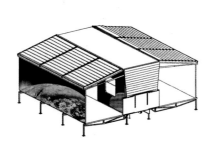
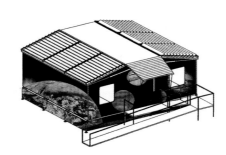
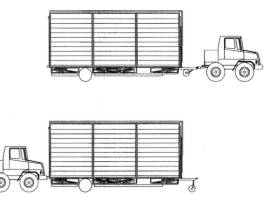
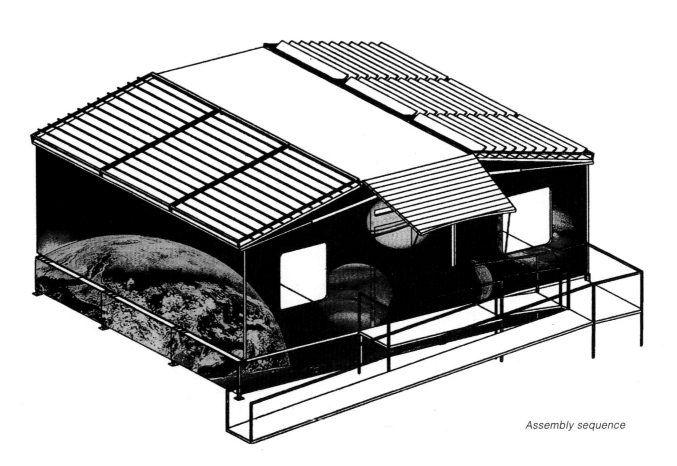

Assembly sequence

FTL HAPPOLD

MOBILE CAMPUS
New York City

In New York City, overcrowding in school facilities has been caused by a sudden surge in the school population. This population surge will move through the school grades, requiring short-term elementary, intermediate and high schools.

To build conventional structures, only to find them unused a few years later, is absurd and wasteful. The school authorities also need 'swing space' – classroom space on-site at existing public school grounds, where students can temporarily be relocated in order that portions of the existing building (a few classrooms at a time) can be evacuated for renovation or upgrading.

In response, the New York City School Construction Authority established the requirement for temporary deployable classrooms that can augment school facilities at a specific location and move on after they are no longer needed.

Current state-of-the-art temporary classrooms consist of double-width mobile home units that are expensive and not truly mobile as they need to be set in place by crane. The environment these facilities provide for education has also been criticised widely.

FTL, in collaboration with the client, has explored the potential for a much better solution to replace the existing so-called 'mobile' classrooms. In addition, the practice has extended the brief so that the new facilities can form an entire campus for 300 students, with classrooms, administration offices, a library, room for art/music, science and computer work, a cafeteria and a gymnasium. These faciliites could also be used in stand-alone situations brought on by emergencies or the programmed refurbishment of an entire school.

A unique aspect of the project is that the buildings are deployed from a staging area (a dedicated trailer truck yard as they are based on modified truck trailers), and are capable of carrying all of their own infrastructure, including power generation, heating and air conditioning, toilets, water storage, fuel storage, etc. This makes them entirely independent of public services and the utility grid. Over a hundred New York City public school sites within a 15-mile radius will be serviced by these wheeled buildings, which will only remain on site as long as they are required.

The prototype design utilises a 25-foot-long semi-trailer with walls that unfold to create a 28 x 25 foot classroom. The expected setup time is approximately 24 hours. Special features, such as exterior walls decorated with dramatic graphics and the luminous fabric roof serve to contradict the notion that a temporary classroom is a poor substitute for the permanent building.

The designers' objectives were to create an appropriate environment for teaching (safe, secure, temperate and well-lit) that could be produced at a lower price than existing equipment. It was also crucial that the image of the portable buildings was identifiable with beneficial change, facilitating the rapid and efficient improvement of the city's existing educational buildings.

Robert Kronenburg

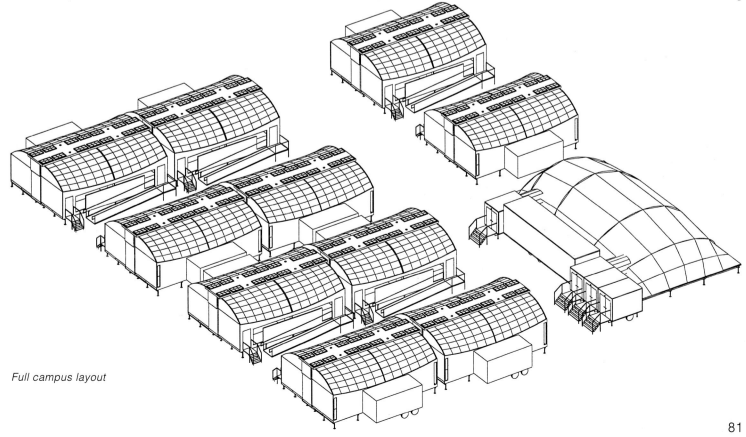

Full campus layout

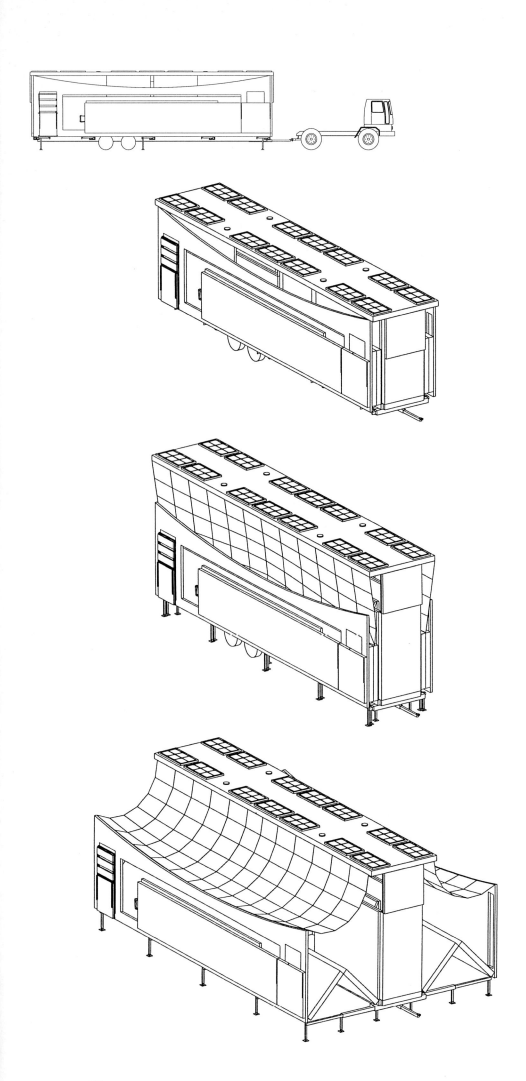
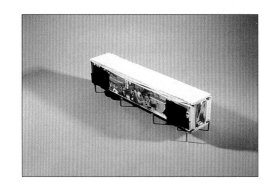
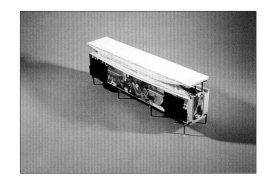
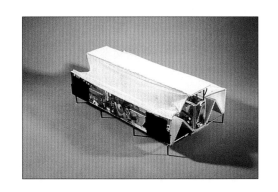

Assembly sequence – semi-trailer to classroom

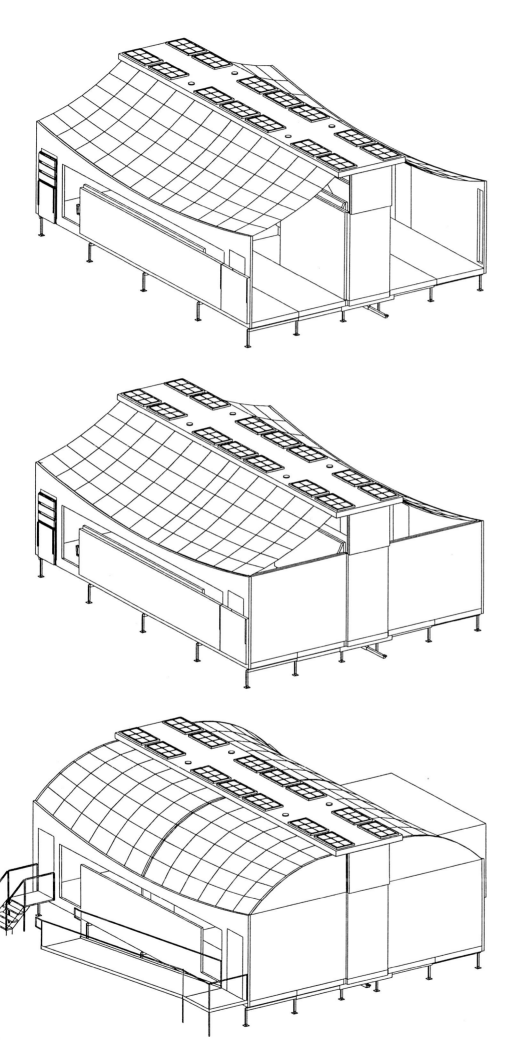

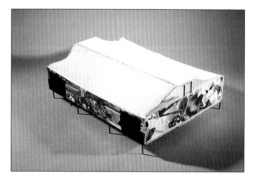
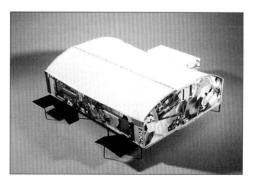

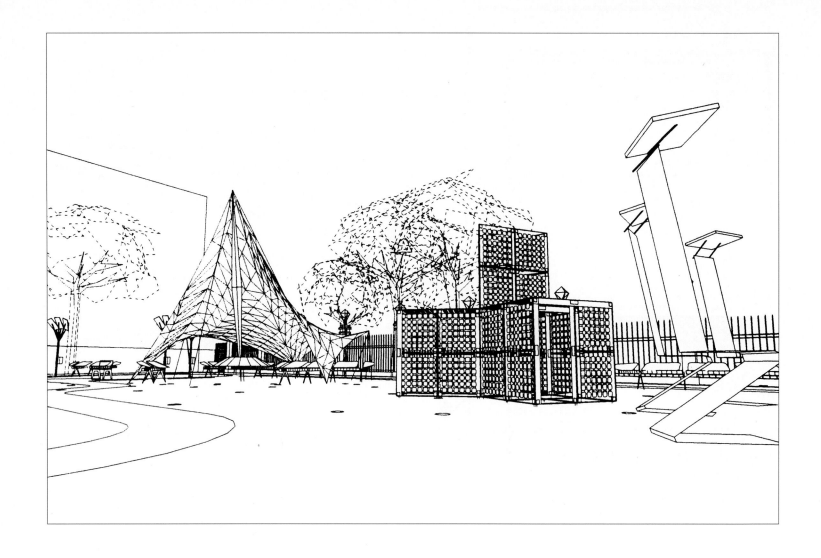

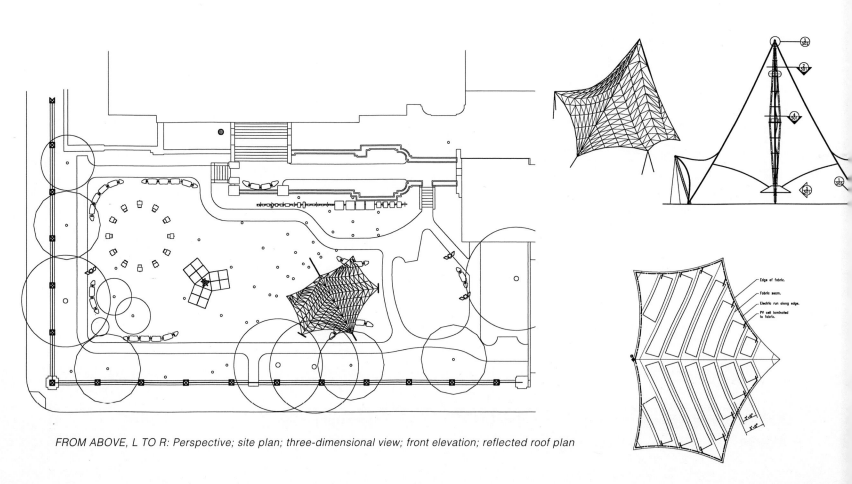

FROM ABOVE, L TO R: Perspective; site plan; three-dimensional view; front elevation; reflected roof plan

FTL HAPPOLD

'UNDER THE SUN' EXHIBITION STRUCTURES
Cooper-Hewitt National Design Museum, New York City

Orientation towards the sun was of paramount importance to the ancient civilisations, as exemplified by the Great Pyramids near Giza, or in the ancient Inca temples of Machu Picchu, where the winter solstice sun illuminated the altar once a year. Not only was the relation of the angle of the sun to their own latitude understood, but the change in angle from the high summer sun to the low winter one. These qualities were universal: societies could not exist without knowledge of the sun.

As civilisations around the world developed, indigenous buildings continued to pay homage to the sun in more subtle ways. However, with the advent of urbanism and its new focus on the street, solar orientation became more difficult to achieve and was often eclipsed by other considerations. Many buildings of the last 100 years are wholly non-site specific; in these cases, the relationship with the sun has been lost completely.

It is only recently that the fundamental importance of using passive and active solar energy in architecture has been resurrected and become of concern to architects and building-services professionals. The development of photovoltaics over the last three decades has dramatically enhanced the potential for convenient use of solar energy. The cost of a new panel today is half of one per cent of a panel of equivalent power 30 years ago. Besides the long used single crystalline and polycrystalline arrays, we now have amorphous silicone and cadmium telluride products – lower priced alternatives which, it is predicted, will allow us to produce electricity at lower costs than mains utility rate within the next 10 years.

Coupled with the recent combination of flexible photovoltaic cells with structural membranes, a new form of light responsive, energy that provides structurally frugal buildings is set to emerge. In essence, we are at a unique moment in time when the evolution of this technology will begin to have a dramatic impact on the lives of buildings and their inhabitants.

The 1998 'Under the Sun' exhibition, designed with Kiss and Cathcart Architects, seeks to highlight the design potential of the new materials and technology. A 32-foot-high tensile structure with flexible thin-film photovoltaic arrays bonded to an architectural shade cloth demonstrates the potential of off-grid power systems.

In developing countries with intensive solar climates, this technology could provide valuable shade and power simultaneously. Electric vehicle batteries could recharge under parking areas covered by these tensile skins, or emergency shelters for disaster relief be provided with instant power.

Another element in the exhibition is a glass pavilion which incorporates 54 photovoltaic modules laminated on to four-foot glass panels which serve as surface, structure and power system. This pavilion demonstrates the use of photovoltaic glass panels as spandrel glass, but also its potential to create transparency levels of up to 30 per cent through the use of laser-scribing of the photovoltaic deposits.

Such buildings have a more intimate relationship with the course of the day and the seasons. While drawing on the technological resources of our age, they reflect the importance of environmental conditions in an interactive way, recalling the harmonious relationship that existed between finely-tuned traditional buildings of the past and the environment.

Nicholas Goldsmith

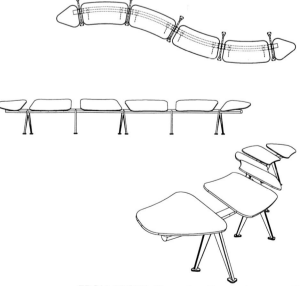

FROM ABOVE: Plan, elevation and perspective of Spline table

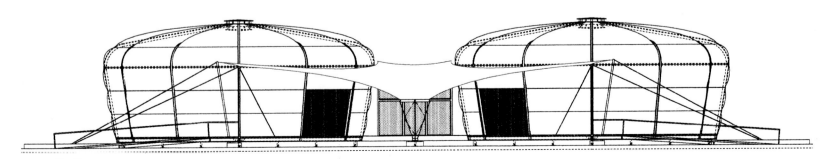

Section

BRANSON COATES ARCHITECTURE

POWERHOUSE::UK

London

Temporary exhibition structures are fertile ground for the exploration of unusual forms in architecture. In this case, the exhibition theme, 'cutting edge design', enhanced the designer's remit to explore the project's potential to the full, but also added the responsibility of creating an appropriate 'cutting edge' building image.

The architectural practice Branson Coates has extensive experience in designing for dramatic effect and image, exemplified not only by exhibition projects such as Living Bridges at the Royal Academy, and Erotic Design at the Design Museum, in London, but also by their Japanese work: for example, the Art Silo and the Wall building.

The commission from the Department of Trade and Industry was to create a showcase of the best of innovative British Design – for presentation primarily to the European and Asian Heads of Government and business attending the ASEM 2 meeting in early April 1998, as well as to the public. The building was to be open for only three weeks with a one-week set-up period and was to include many different aspects of innovative design expertise: computer graphics, media special effects, automotive design, genetic engineering and furniture design.

The site at Horse Guard's Parade is a high-profile destination, on tourism agendas for the daily ritual of Changing of the Guard and special events each June when it forms the setting for Beating the Retreat and Trooping the Colour. The ceremonial nature of the site makes it especially suitable for temporary structures, which must attract visitors not only by their advance publicity but by being adjacent to a recognisable 'address'. The range of traditional formal government buildings that formed the backdrop to Powerhouse::UK was an interesting foil to the exhibition's transient and dynamic nature.

The structure was composed of four 16-metre-diameter drums, positioned symmetrically around a central crossing in response to the symmetry of the site. The symmetry was enhanced further by four ramps leading towards a central circulation space, providing visitors with the choice of visiting the exhibition areas in any order. Each of the spaces focused on one area of creativity – lifestyle, communication, learning, networking –although the exhibits themselves expressed the interconnectivity of the design process.

The steel-framed structure was clad in silver coloured, inflated fabric, matched by the exhibition hostesses' silver 'Michelin

Man' jackets. In darkness, the building glowed from within, gently illuminating Horse Guard's Parade and the surrounding, comparatively sombre buildings.

One problem of large-scale temporary buildings is that they cannot make use of conventional foundations either for support or restraint. In this case, engineering consultants Buro Happold advised that the four ramps be made of concrete to anchor the building against wind loads. The main steel structure used simple sections and connections to avoid complicated erection processes.

The membrane was inflated with small electric fans and connected to the steel ribs with extruded aluminium sections. A tensile membrane covered the central space using well-tested fabric structure detailing to accommodate both tensile forces to maintain its shape and rigidity and imposed compression forces resulting from wind load.

The main design requirements for the Powerhouse::UK exhibition were that it be easy and quick to erect and dismantle, and economic to manufacture. This resulted in a building that was comparatively heavy for a temporary structure – 60 tonnes in the steel work alone, a fact which is at odds with its apparent lightweight image

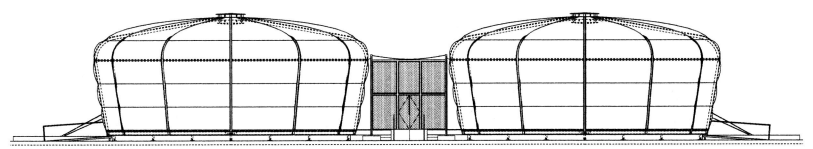

Elevation

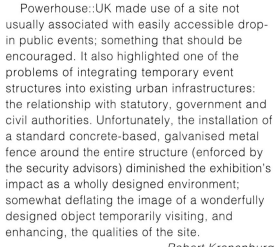

Powerhouse::UK made use of a site not usually associated with easily accessible drop-in public events; something that should be encouraged. It also highlighted one of the problems of integrating temporary event structures into existing urban infrastructures: the relationship with statutory, government and civil authorities. Unfortunately, the installation of a standard concrete-based, galvanised metal fence around the entire structure (enforced by the security advisors) diminished the exhibition's impact as a wholly designed environment; somewhat deflating the image of a wonderfully designed object temporarily visiting, and enhancing, the qualities of the site.

Robert Kronenburg

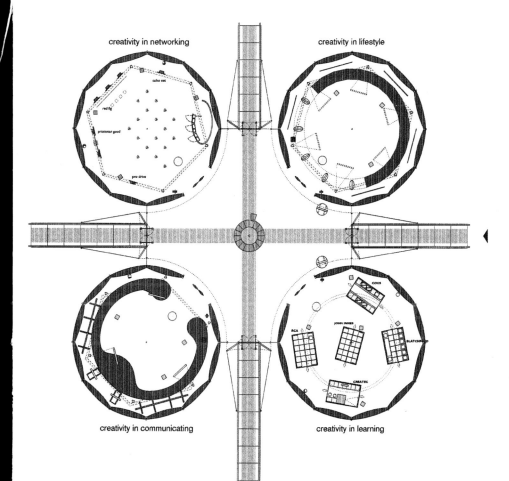

creativity in networking

creativity in lifestyle

creativity in communicating

creativity in learning

WENDY GUNN AND GAVIN RENWICK
'WHAUR EXTREMES MEET'

I'll ha'e nae huaf-way hoose, but aye be whaur
Extremes meet – it's the only way I ken
To dodge the curst conceit o' being right
That damns the vast majority o' men.
Hugh MacDiarmid, 'A Drunk Man Looks
at the Thistle', 1926

'Whaur Extremes Meet' functioned as a
meeting point for different opinions: a
place for the mutual illumination of blind
spots, to use George Davies' expression
(1986). In the words of Murdo MacDonald,

> It was an instant college building in
> the sense of a place where a com-
> pany of people can congregate,
> essentially provisional (i.e. meeting
> necessity) in a society in which
> channels of communication between
> people have either been severed or
> have became clogged with irrel-
> evancies. (1990, *Variant*)

The structure, through being recognised
for its purpose rather than its appearance,
enabled people to wander in and out,
participating in a conversation of which
their own circumstances were part. It

facilitated meaningful and relevant
conversation about their city without the
usual constraints of pre-existing bureauc-
racies and institutions. Specialists and
politicians were involved but only through
recognising that they had no special power
there and their roles were open to scrutiny,
not only by others but by themselves.

The collaborative team recognised the
restrictions of conducting debates
according to conventional polarities and
attempted to challenge environmental
perceptions that posit these elements as
irreconcilable (art or architecture, aes-
thetics or technology, tradition or modernity,
freedom or society, rural or urban).

This bio-climatic discussion forum was
designed and constructed in Istanbul. It
was assembled, dissembled and transported overland, and built in Athens,
Belgrade, Budapest, Prague, Berlin and
finally Glasgow. It acted as a catalyst by
providing a focus for formal discussions.
Additional events and workshops were
organised by the inhabitants of each city;
ranging, for example in Istanbul, from a

local council meeting (one of many
convened in the structure) to a performance art group utilising the structure as a
framework for a public performance.

The formal discussions included 'The
Effects of Rural Migration', in Istanbul;
'Environment and the City', in Athens;
'Nationalism v Internationalism', in
Belgrade; 'A National Architectural
Language?', in Budapest; 'The Effects of
Totalitarianism on City Planning', in
Prague; 'The Development of Potsdamer
Platz', in Berlin; and in Glasgow, 'The
Design of Public Space' and 'Community
Involvement in the Design Process'.

Research for the project was conducted
initially in the Cankurtaran area of Istanbul,
where the project team lived and worked.
The area is situated between the Sea of
Marmara and Sultanahmet, bounded by
sea and the walls of the Topkapi Palace.
During 1989 and 1990, the inhabitants
were mainly from the Black Sea and
Eastern Anatolian regions of Turkey. The
site's geographical isolation from the city
gave it an autonomy and sense of com-

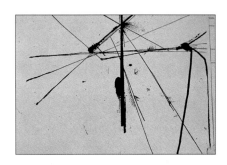

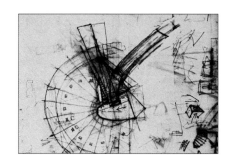
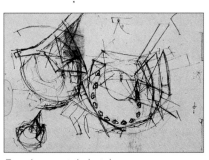
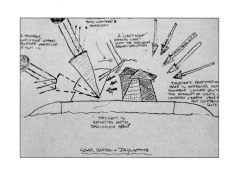

Developmental sketches

munity that defied its social isolation by the Istanbul bourgeoisie.

Conventional design briefs seem to encourage the abstract definition of space and isolation of function, over a design that evolves from an investigation of the social processes of surrounding context, the realities (the potentials) of climate, the process of habitation. The impetus, development, design and programming of this project was therefore entirely collaborative and specific to context.

The team developed an intuitive understanding of each given public place in the project's locations, through research and documentation of the processes of habitation and movement patterns. Our then naive optimism drove the idea of collaboration to a logical conclusion, defying our specialisms and attempting to negate our professional egos through developing the design by drawing in unison; consciously attempting to challenge the quantitative methodology and metric measurements that conventionally describe and conceive environment

through impersonalised abstract theory.

By extending the collaboration to include a structural and environmental engineer, from project sponsors Ove Arup & Partners and local crafts-people at a relatively early stage in the design development, environmental and structural technologies that remained responsive to context were integrated. The task was to develop an appropriate technology that was responsive to seven locations that were physically, culturally and climatically diverse, while meeting the restrictions of a limited budget.

Essentially a day structure, having no electricity, artificial heating, cooling or lighting, its servicing was self-contained and autonomous from any generated energy source in each city. Its fragmented construction was adaptable to the different climates encountered. Adjustable louvres controlled the light and solar gain to the internal space, permitting wind to pass through the structure; aiding stability in adverse weather conditions while still allowing

visual and audio contact between the group and passing public. Gaps between each segment afforded air movement in order to alleviate heat radiation inwards.

Learning from Turkoman nomads, water-filled tanks encircled the structure, providing counterweight and climate control. The stack effect of the design was used to draw air and evaporation through the structure.

Sponsorship and research funding for the project included: The European Cultural Foundation, The British Council, The Scottish Arts Council, Strathclyde Regional Council, Glasgow District Council, Eminonu Belediyesi, Ove Arup & Partners, Emlak Bankasi, John Walker & Sons and British Rail International.

Gavin Renwick

Based on a paper presented to the First International Conference on Portable Architecture in London, May 1997, the proceedings of which will be published in Transportable Environments, *E&FN Spon (London), late 1998*

BIOGRAPHIES

Lorenzo Apicella studied architecture at Nottingham University, Canterbury College of Art and the Royal College of Art in London before working for Skidmore, Owings and Merrill in the USA. From 1986 he was head of architecture and interior design at Imagination in London and in 1989 he founded the design and architecture practice Apicella Associates. He is currently a visiting lecturer at the Graduate School of Architecture at Oxford Brookes University; External Examiner to the School of Design at UCE Birmingham; a Fellow of the Chartered Society of Designers, and a Fellow of the Royal Society of Arts.

Branson Coates Architecture is based in London and was set-up by Doug Branson and Nigel Coates in 1985. Branson studied and taught architecture at Canterbury College of Art and Architecture, and the Architectural Association in London, where Coates taught from 1976-86. Coates has lectured abroad extensively and in 1995 was appointed Professor of Architectural Design at the Royal College of Art. The team has a strong reputation for innovative exhibition and gallery design; recent projects include the extension to the Geffrye Museum in London, the National Centre for Popular Music in Sheffield, and the design of the *Living Bridges* exhibition at the Royal Academy in London.

Nicholas Goldsmith studied architecture at Cornell University in the USA. After working with Frei Otto in Germany, he returned to the USA to join his partner Todd Dalland in the formation of the architecture/engineering practice FTL, specialising in the design and construction of innovative buildings utilising tensile membranes. The practice has designed many major projects across the Eastern seaboard of the USA and was one of the major designers of the 1996 Atlanta Olympic Games. A monograph on their work *FTL: Softness Movement and Light* was published by Academy Editions in 1997. Goldsmith is a fellow of the AIA and teaches at the University of Pennsylvania.

Toyo Ito was born in Seoul, Korea, and graduated in architecture from the University of Tokyo in 1965. Since 1971, he has been in private architectural practice, based in Tokyo. He is well-known for buildings and structures which helped establish a new wave of significant Japanese architecture such as the Tower of the Winds (1986), the Egg of Winds (1989), and the Sapporo Guesthouse (1989).

Günter Zamp Kelp was a pivotal founding member of the experimental architect/artist group Haus-Rucker-Co. This was founded in Vienna in 1967 (with Laurids Ortner and Klaus Pinter, and Manfred Ortner from 1971) and continued until 1992. In 1987 he established his independent practice in Düsseldorf. He is also a professor of architecture at the Hochschule Der Kunste in Berlin.

Robert Kronenburg is an architect and director of studies of the Bachelor of Architecture course at the School of Architecture, University of Liverpool, UK. His recent design and research work has concentrated on the field of lightweight, temporary and portable architecture. His books include *Houses in Motion: The Genesis, History and Development of the Portable Building*, published by Academy Editions, and *Portable Architecture*. In 1997, he curated the Portable Architecture exhibition at the RIBA Architecture Centre in London. He is currently editing *Transportable Environments*, a book of international essays to be published by E&FN Spon late in 1998.

Vladimir Krstic is an Associate Professor of Architecture at Kansas State University. He lived in Japan for a number of years studying architecture and working with Tadao Ando Architect & Associates. His academic research centres on urban design theory: in particular, the Japanese contemporary city and the ways in which the dynamism of its formal, physical and meaning-generating configuration is influencing the conceptual re-structuring of architecture

Joep van Lieshout and Klaar van der Lippe are both artists, living and working in Rotterdam, who have collaborated on several projects. Van Lieshout gained international recognition in 1994 through design work for the Grand Palais, Lille, with architect Rem Koolhaas. In 1995 he established the Rotterdam based Atelier van Lieshout. Van Lieshout's work ranges from furniture design to sculpture and environmental installations.

Henrietta Palmer is an architect and post-graduate teacher at the Royal University of Fine Arts, Department of Architecture, Stockholm. Recently, her specialist theme has been the exploration of architecture, cities and tourism.

Mark Prizeman is an architectural teacher and practitioner who works in London. He was trained at the Architectural Association in London. He teaches there, alongside architecture courses at the University of East London.

Gavin Renwick and Wendy Gunn collaborate on self-generated and commissioned projects, exhibitions, and pedagogic practice, and are independently involved in academic research. Gavin Renwick is affiliated to the Design Department of Napier University, Edinburgh, and is currently undertaking both research and practice on the house and home in Canada's sub-Arctic, based in Yellowknife, Northwest Territories. Wendy Gunn is now based within the Department of Social Anthropology at the University of Manchester, and is currently involved in field work in Tromso, northern Norway, concerned with the social and environmental impact of incorporating CAD technology into the architecture design process.

Torsten Schmiedeknecht studied architecture in Darmstadt, Paris and London. He has practised architecture in Greece, France, the UK, and Germany. His work with Gerhard Knapp resulted in several commendations and prizes in architecture and fine art competitions and he is currently involved in architectural practice at the Office for Architecture, London. He is a part-time lecturer and studio tutor at the School of Architecture, University of Liverpool and is conducting research into the experimental group of Austrian artists/architects Haus-Rucker-Co.